LIBERALIZATION IN THE USSR:
FACADE OR REALITY?

PROBLEMS IN POLITICAL SCIENCE
under the editorial direction of NEAL RIEMER, *University of Wisconsin-Milwaukee*

OTHER VOLUMES IN PREPARATION

Liberalization in the USSR:

FACADE OR REALITY?

EDITED WITH AN INTRODUCTION BY

D. Richard Little
Northern Illinois University

D. C. Heath and Company
A DIVISION OF RAYTHEON EDUCATION COMPANY
LEXINGTON, MASSACHUSETTS

FOR LINDA

320.082
H437
v. 4

Table of Contents

v

The Clash of Ideas

THE QUESTION OF DEMOCRACY

For someone who has been chastised with scorpions for any length of time, it is no doubt quite a relief to have the chastiser go back to whips again. And it would be quite false to ignore the change for the better in Soviet conditions. Yet a double objection still remains: First, whips are unpleasant enough. Second—and in some ways a more cogent objection—Soviet society remains divided into the whippers and the whipped, and the whippers retain the right to decide what form the relationship between the two shall take in the future.

—ROBERT CONQUEST

A sharp break occurred a decade ago with the removal of Stalin from the pedestal of deity. . . . This is the change from dictatorship to consensus, in which the Party is now the agency through which the organized structures of a stable and complex society, showing unmistakable signs of a pluralist mechanism, arrive at a set of working policies.

—WILLIAM M. MANDEL

THE NEW ELITES

The [technological] experts, in short, are servants rather than masters or even independent practitioners. They lack the power of veto on grounds of technical rationality over political decisions. . . . And their potential for independent influence in society is decisively cut short by the elite's consistent practice of defining *all* decision-making as political and therefore beyond the competence of any group other than itself.

—ALLEN KASSOF

Powerful interest groups have shown remarkable stubbornness in clinging to their opinions. . . . The Soviet government cannot function without using these groups; it cannot make sensible decisions without their advice, and it cannot get that advice without allowing some discussion of basic issues.

—JOSEPH R. STRAYER

COERCION AND THE LAW

The restoration of procedural due process of law in political cases is a signal achievement of the post–Stalin regime. The Soviet citizen is now protected against police terror, false charges, and faked trials to a far greater extent than ever before in Soviet history. No longer need he fear the midnight knock on the door as a prelude to transportation to a Siberian Labor camp without a fair hearing.

—HAROLD BERMAN

Soviet law and judicial policy may be less of a mockery than they were under Stalin, but it remains true—as the preamble to the new law on "state crimes" makes clear—that they are still based "on the need for *the greatest possible* defense of . . . [the] state." Indeed, Soviet jurists are still disputing the very legitimacy of recognizing the defense of the rights of citizens as one of the functions of law.

—JEREMY R. AZRAEL

EQUALITY AND DISCRIMINATION

In general, the party seems to have been going out of its way . . . to raise the ordinary worker's self-respect, and to imbue him with the consciousness—denied him under Stalin—of his own contribution to the country's industrial progress.

—ROBERT A. FELDMESSER

In the field of nationality relations, [the party's] policy has entailed a more pronounced subordination of the interests and aspirations of the individual nationalities to the interests of the Soviet Union and its predominant ethnic group, the Russians.

—YAROSLAV BILINSKY

Introduction

The propensity of social movements and institutions to change their nature over time is probably the only unalterable characteristic of the social order. Yet there are times when change surprises us, when we are unprepared for it both intellectually and emotionally, especially when it occurs in social systems accepted as permanent and durable by a generation or two of scholarly observers. The recent history of the Soviet political system is a case in point. For nearly a quarter of a century, until his death in 1953, Joseph Stalin dominated Russia more thoroughly, and altered the course of her development more profoundly, than even the most powerful of the seventeen Romanov Czars and Czarinas who preceded him. Having seized the levers of power in the late 1920's, Stalin used them to eliminate his rivals, to squelch all controversies over policy matters (since these were interpreted as covert attempts to overthrow Stalin), and to enshroud the whole political process in an almost impenetrable curtain of secrecy.

The success and longevity of Stalin's rule seemed to cast Soviet politics into a permanent mold, characterized by mass obedience to the leader's will, infused with terror, and closed to the tempering influences of time and evolution. Yet the Soviet system in the 1960's presents an image strikingly different from that of the monistic, personalized dictatorship of the previous era. This transformation manifests itself in at least four ways: first, despite the apparent supremacy of Nikita Khrushchev from 1957 to 1964, the post–Stalinist period has been marked by unabated political struggle reflecting a severe degree of disunity and disarray within the party leadership. Secondly, the nature of this conflict has centered far more around major policy questions, and less around the purely personal aspects of the struggle for leadership and power, than previously. The past fifteen years have been a time of radical experimentation in many important areas of public policy. Indeed, the failure of some of the experiments was clearly one of the major causes for the overthrow of Khrushchev in October 1964.

A third factor has been the emergence of political controversy into the public arena. Virtually all aspects of domestic public policy

1

are now debated widely in the press and in professional journals despite the continued dominance of the Communist Party leadership in the decision-making process. Outsiders now even have access to stenographic transcripts of plenary meetings of the Party Central Committee. Finally, the relaxation of terror, and a consequent increase in the psychological sense of well-being, are unmistakable in contemporary Soviet society.

Taking cognizance of these changes, a number of Western scholars have attempted to analyze the nature of post-Stalinist Soviet society in terms of whether or not these and other developments constitute a genuine *liberalization* of the Soviet system. The ensuing controversy, which is reflected in the essays in this book, has focussed not only on political developments, but on the whole pattern of social, economic, scientific, ideological, and intellectual developments which have taken place during the past decade and a half.

Part of the difficulty in resolving the controversy lies in the semantic connotations of the term *liberalization*. Often it is used to mean merely the "easing" or "relaxation" of police controls over the lives and thoughts of the Soviet people, particularly in contrast to the harshness of the Stalinist era. Thus the closing of the notorious Siberian labor camps, of which Alexander Solzhenitsin has written so eloquently, is sometimes considered evidence of liberalization, along with the increasing production of consumer goods, introduction of the 40-hour week, and the disbanding of the machine-tractor stations. Used in this way, the term becomes so diffuse that very little that has happened in the Soviet Union since 1953 could *not* be included within the meaning of the term.

On the other hand, some observers take a much narrower view of the term, arguing that only substantial progress toward the dissolution of the party's political monopoly and the establishment of a representative, parliamentary democracy in its place would constitute genuine liberalization. Since this seems obviously not in prospect, they then discount the possibility of liberalization. It is more difficult to reject this view, for the establishment of democratic governments, universal suffrage, and the protection of civil rights are certainly fundamental to the Western liberal tradition. One can argue, therefore, that if the term is to have any consistent, generally accepted meaning, it must be applied to Russia in the same way.

Despite this type of reasoning, the application of this definition of *liberalization* to the Soviet Union is inappropriate. The fault lies largely in the assumptions underlying the concept of Western liberalism. The use of the term today generally refers to the *end result* of nearly two centuries of development, deflecting attention from the long, slow process by which liberal ideas came to dominate most of the Western political systems. Yet if the Russian experience can be compared with any validity to the development of Western liberalism, it must be compared to the earlier struggles and setbacks, rather than to the values and institutions of contemporary liberal societies. Furthermore, the phrase "Western European liberalism" obscures the great diversity of political systems established in Europe under the impact of liberal ideas, and tends to focus on the Anglo–American states, in which liberalism struck deeper roots than it did in the continental countries. As George Sabine points out, "only in England . . . did liberalism achieve the status at once of a national philosophy and a rational policy." To compare Russian development only to the special brand of liberalism established in England and the United States is to restrict unnecessarily the possibility of meaningful comparison.

A further difficulty in comparing Russian with Western liberalism is that the Western liberal movement was not satisfied with small gains, but aimed at, and gradually achieved, a profound transformation in the political philosophy and governmental systems of the Western world. In Russia, the liberal movement consistently put forth more modest demands, at least until at the turn of the century it finally became evident to many liberals that only the overthrow of the autocracy would bring about significant change. When this happened, large numbers of liberal intellectual leaders (Miliukov, for example) defected to the revolutionary ranks, rendering Russian liberalism weak and ineffective.

The forces for reform in contemporary Russia are similarly confined to a narrow area. Like their liberal forerunners, they are faced on one side by a powerful and illiberal regime and on the other by the certain knowledge that even modest attempts to effect basic political reforms would expose them to the charge of revolutionary (i.e., anti–party) activity. The agenda for liberalization in the Soviet Union therefore includes a list of reforms far more limited than one normally associates with the full development of Western liberalism, but which is nonetheless highly significant within the historical context of Russian development.

Two examples may help to clarify the point. In the West, especially in England and the United States, the struggle for freedom of speech and press was pursued on a total basis. In the present century in particular, the major issue has been whether or not considerations of social propriety, national interest, and the power of the printed and spoken word to evoke action (as in the "clear and present danger" test) can be used to justify limitations on free speech. It has generally been assumed that speech should be unencumbered by restrictions except where such overriding justifications could be demonstrated. In Russia, the issue was never phrased this extensively even by liberals, nor is this the issue in contemporary Soviet society. Here the issue has traditionally revolved around narrower and more fundamental questions: whether public opinion should be expressed at all, even in approval of the government (a dispute resolved by Nicholas I with a total silencing of public opinion); whether works of fiction should be excluded from the generally accepted right of the government to censure publications (a major issue for the Bolshevik government as well as for czarist regimes); and whether recourse to the courts should be available in cases of violation of censorship laws.

A second example involves the concept of pluralism, a notion valued by liberals in Russia as well as in the West. But in Russia the idea took a peculiar form. Russian society, before as well as after the Revolution, has been characterized by the absence of what Robert Dahl calls "sub-system autonomy"—the ability of political parties, interest groups, and the media of mass communication to function independently of governmental and bureaucratic control. Since Peter the Great transformed the nobility into a kind of royal civil service in the early eighteenth century, no major social, religious, or economic group has performed an autonomous political role as in the West. As a result, the question of pluralism in Russia is not how much such groups should influence the processes of government, but whether they should exist at all. It is essential therefore to view changes in modern Soviet society in a Russian, rather than a Western, context. Small advances toward a liberalized Russia in the present era are no less significant than similar small advances were in the West a century ago.

One further definitional problem arises from the fact that liberalism has historically been associated with the rise of democratic institutions in Europe and the United States. This has led some observers, as mentioned above, to judge Soviet liberalization solely on evidence of political democratization. This view ignores the fact that throughout most of the nineteenth century the freedom demanded by liberals was not accompanied by similar demands for total political democracy, and this was true in Russia as well as in the West. As George Fischer has pointed out, referring to mid-nineteenth century Russia: "Most of the gentry liberals . . . shared with most Western liberals of this period the apprehensions about unqualified democracy and large-scale social reforms. And they admired Western parliaments and constitutions without being certain when and how they might be transplanted to Russia." It is easily forgotten that in England—the seedbed of liberalism—the Tories broadened the franchise more often than the liberal Whigs, and that the last vestige of weighted voting was not eliminated in England until 1945. In the Soviet Union, liberalization may be occurring, as it did in the West, far in advance of the development of political democracy. Although this is possible, it is still true that a totally undemocratic society could hardly be a very liberal one. Thus the controversy over liberalization necessarily involves attention to the development of democratic institutions and practices in the Soviet Union, if such there be.

With the above reflections in mind, the following definition of liberalization is offered for purposes of the present discussion:

a) A meaningful increase in the participation of the citizenry, both as a whole and through discrete interest groups, in the decision-making processes of the government;

b) An increasing measure of institutionalized protection of Soviet citizens in the exercise of constitutional rights, particularly freedom of speech and opinion and the right of equal treatment under law;

c) A political climate increasingly amenable to cultural and intellectual freedom, and free of discrimination among citizens on the basis of occupation, creed, or nationality.

To a contemporary Western liberal, these would be, at best, barely minimal components of a liberal society. But in the Soviet context they attain far greater significance when compared with the total absence of liberal ideals during the quarter century of Stalin's rule. This list is in no sense exhaustive—general agreement on a precise definition of *liberalization* would probably be impossible to achieve—but positive developments in at least these three areas would be a significant development in the direction of a more liberal Soviet Union. The four groups of selections in this volume present conflicting conclusions, based on a wide diversity of evidence, which relate to the three components of *liberalization* stated above.

Popular Participation in the Political Process

The revolutionary ferment which embroiled nineteenth-century Europe followed the banner of "democracy" as an ideal, a symbol, a magic sword with which to sever the Gordian knot of poverty, oppression and injustice. In its more radical form, the European social democratic movement pursued a kind of communal anarchy where popular self-government would make it possible to dispense with governments, police, and the bureaucratic arrogance associated with all organized states, and to substitute a Rousseauean consensus in which all men would share. In this form, the notion of democracy was absorbed by the Russian Bolshevik movement in the waning years of the nineteenth century. Its vitality (as an ideal, at least) is attested to by its appearance in the 1961 Party Program, phrased almost the same as at the turn of the century.

Nevertheless, the reality of the post-revolutionary Soviet regime bore little resemblance to this ideal. The economic and social tasks established by Stalin in the late 1920's were far too dramatic and urgent to permit the revolutionary state to suffer the endemic gradualism of Western-type democracy. This, coupled with the paranoic drive for power exhibited by Stalin himself, eliminated any practical manifestation of the democratic ideal during the period of Stalin's rule. It is a perennial source of dispute among scholars (both Western and Communist) as to whether the roots of Stalinism lay more fundamentally in the personality of the despot or in the objective requirements of modernizing and industrializing a backward nation with the greatest possible speed, in the face of a hostile and dangerous world. What is important to the present discussion, however, is that neither of these two elements persists as a dominant factor in the contemporary Soviet system. Despite the continued presence of Stalinists in high party positions and the weakness of agriculture and certain other economic enterprises, the death of Stalin and the modernization and industrialization of the Soviet Union are accomplished facts which have profoundly altered the environment in which the governmental system operates. Let us consider these two developments separately.

Since 1953, a crisis of legitimacy has settled upon the party leadership as a result of the absence of a single, unifying center of authority formerly provided by Stalin. Khrushchev's "de-stalinization" speech in 1956 seriously weakened the party's claim to omniscience, not only in regard to public policies, but in terms of the selection of party leaders as well. The fact that every party leader since Lenin has been publicly discredited by his successor has raised the spector of illegitimacy both within the party ranks and within the population at large. Khrushchev's growing awareness of this crisis induced him to seek broader bases of support from lower level party organizations and from the masses of Soviet citizens. Hence the "Leninist" revival of "public participation" in the affairs of government and the dedication to "collective leadership" which is so loudly trumpeted as the supreme principle of Soviet democracy.

The insistent question, in light of these developments, is whether the novel practices instituted by the regime to increase popular participation in the political process really amount to a diffusion of responsibility for public policy and a commitment by the leadership, however reluctant, to more liberal forms of rule; or whether on the other hand, the changes amount to nothing more than the evolution to a less primitive and more palatable form of totalitarianism.

The latter view is presented by Robert Conquest. He argues that the outstanding quality of the Soviet political system, with or without Stalin, has always been the exercise of an oppressive dictatorship by a non-elective ruling elite. It is true, he concedes, that the degree of regimentation and coercion in Soviet society has diminished somewhat since the death of Stalin. But "to equate this with anything approaching democratization is completely erroneous." In contrast to this view, both T. H. Rigby and William M. Mandel find meaningful democratic values and practices both within the party and in the society at large. While not denying the profoundly anti-democratic character of Stalinism, Rigby contends that the Bolshevik movement, as distinct from its individual leaders, has always displayed an inclination toward reviving democratic procedures whenever internal conditions make it possible. "It seems," he points out, "that the majority of party members take the 'democratic' part [of 'democratic centralism'] seriously and while aware of the 'limitations' in practice, tend to accept these limitations as a temporary necessity."

Mandel's view of the political process is based upon what he believes to be a major transformation "from dictatorship to consensus, in which the party is now the agency through which the

organized structures of a stable and complex society, showing unmistakable signs of a pluralist mechanism, arrive at a set of working policies." For the government, this means a revival of the state
as distinct from the party apparatus; for the citizen, it introduces
"a vast amount of participatory democracy on many vital subjects."
Neither Rigby nor Mandel views the Soviet system as democratic
in the full sense of the word. But, in contrast to Conquest, they
identify elements of democracy which they believe to be an important and developing quality of the Soviet autocracy.

The New Elites and the Development of Pluralism
The second major development of the post-Stalinist era is the
Soviet Union's emergence as the second greatest industrial state in
the world, supported by a largely urban population, almost universal literacy, practically inexhaustible resources, and a military
machine fully capable of protecting the state's new-found wealth
and status. In the wake of this development has come a loosening
and expanding of the elite structure which formerly dominated the
state, and with it an increasing diversity of interests, values, and
viewpoints directed toward policy decisions of the party leadership.

To an extent, such diversity is no doubt a natural reaction to
the decrease in terror and police control begun soon after Stalin's
death. But it has other roots as well, more directly associated with
the developmental processes under way. Rapid industrialization, re-
quiring more specialized skills for managers, technicians, and party
officials, produced a far more complex division of labor than had
existed in the 1930's. As the educational system supplied men with
these skills, new conflicts developed, particularly between loyalty
to the leader and his policies and the subordinate loyalties which
men naturally give to their families, their occupations, their skills
and talents, and their need for self-preservation and advancement.
"Men are preoccupied by their skills," David Truman has written,
"and these preoccupations in large measure define what the members of such groups know and perceive about the world in which
they live." The fact that the Communist Party wields ultimate
power in the state does not necessarily indicate that its ideals,
values, and perspectives are the literal convictions of all subordinate
sectors of society. In recent years the party's demand for unity
and discipline has come increasingly into conflict with the gradual
crystallization of an interest-group structure whose views and concerns often diverge from those of the party leadership. Furthermore, the evident lack of unity within the party elite on basic

issues has afforded various interest groups strategic allies in the highest circles of power.

These developments are subjected to critical examination in the selections in Part II of this volume. Allen Kassof and Joseph Strayer present opposite views of the potential for pluralistic development within the Soviet system. Kassof points to what he calls the "remarkable success of the Soviet regime" in protecting its monopoly of political power, preventing the formation of independent interest–group cohesion, and manipulating the democratic state institutions so as to prevent their becoming a focal point for pluralistic pressures. "Ironically," he concludes, "the regime is probably correct . . . when it insists that any form of pluralism is impossible."

Strayer is far less impressed with the party's long–term ability to preserve its prestige and power intact. This is both because of the inability of the current leadership to appropriate to itself the combination of admiration and fear which the Soviet people exhibited toward Stalin, and because of the party's greatly increased dependence on technological experts to resolve social and economic problems. For the sake of its own programs, the party has been forced to open the door to widespread public discussion of basic policy questions, thus broadening considerably the participation of groups and individuals in the policy–making process. Strayer goes so far as to suggest that even mass public opinion, "nebulous, unorganized and powerless though it be," is coming to play a more important role in the overall policy perspectives of the party leadership.

Probably the most dramatic changes in the past few years have occurred in the economic system, where a thoroughgoing reform has been instigated. Michel Tatu's analysis of this reform focusses on the opposition it has generated, including many economic planners and most of the major party leaders. The opposition has been based upon "the attachment of many planners to the prevailing administrative methods and the fears within the party over a possible weakening of its prerogatives . . . ." Nevertheless, the reform decisions of September, 1965, represent, in Tatu's words, "a handsome victory for the reformers." It was a limited victory, to be sure, the terms of which "do not . . . even begin to eliminate the fundamental deficiencies of Soviet economic management." But it demonstrates the capacity of liberalizing elements to work openly and relatively effectively against stubborn resistance within the planning establishment and the party leadership.

Coercion, Persuasion, and the Rule of Law

The second point in our definition of liberalization concerns increased protection of the rights of citizens and increased immunity from unlawful or excessive coercion. The selections by Harold Berman and Leonard Schapiro point out a basic source of disagreement on these issues. Both writers identify important liberal reforms of recent years, and both also describe retrogressive developments in the same period. Where they take issue is on the *permanency*, or "institutionalization", of these progressive steps. For Schapiro, "institutionalization" is primarily a structural concept referring to the development of state agencies and offices, such as a constitutional court exercising judicial review, which can operate effectively outside the control of the party. For Berman, the term would apply to the general acceptance of certain values and legal principles, with or without corresponding legal structures to apply them. He identifies a long list of recent changes in legal norms, including adoption of the principle that confessions no longer have special evidentiary force, acceptance of a "presumption of innocence" in criminal cases, and the protection of citizens against "police terror, false charges, and faked trials to a far greater extent than ever before in Soviet history."

The embodiment of such principles in regular judicial institutions would no doubt represent a higher level of institutionalization than their mere acceptance by a group—even a majority—of jurists, lawyers, and laymen. Yet the decades of Soviet rule in which these principles were totally absent provide a sharp contrast to developments of the past few years. It goes without saying that what remains to be done before the Soviet system is operating under the "rule of law" far outweighs what has already been done. Yet both Schapiro and Berman both express a cautious optimism regarding the future of the role of law in the Soviet system.

Legal sanctions are, of course, only one of the instruments by which the party attempts to control public behavior. Even if we can observe a degree of liberalization in the legal processes, this is important only insofar as the behavior of Soviet citizens falls within the jurisdiction of the regular judicial processes. But where that behavior is subject to extra- or non-judicial judgments, the liberalizing effect of legal reforms may be seriously blunted. That this is in fact happening, and increasingly so, is the core of Jeremy Azrael's contention that the level of coercion is rising in the Soviet Union.

Azrael's documentation includes a lengthy list of governmental policies and actions which constitute coercion of the Soviet citizen, including prosecution for political crimes, intimidation by the secret police, assignment to compulsory labor in outlying areas of the country, manipulation of public organizations to enforce public obedience, and "latent coercion" in the form of threats. The question of "coercion" adds psychological and moral dimensions to the subject of liberalization. As regards the morality (or immorality) of coercion, one necessarily starts with the assumption that all governments, liberal or otherwise, in a sense coerce their citizens by enforcing compliance with regulations to which the citizens may individually object. The real question, then, is the *justification* for coercion. Azrael implicitly argues that the kinds of coercion he describes are morally unjustifiable since they "seem clearly to contravene the principles of constitutional democracy and the standards ordinarily observed in constitutional–democratic politics." While it is reasonably certain that most Americans would object to the practices Azrael describes, in the context of Soviet development the matter may not be so clear–cut. Is it more coercive, for example, to assign young Soviets to compulsory labor to promote production than to conscript young Americans for national defense? It is essentially a moral judgment whether military power is more important than economic development under all circumstances—whether conscription for one is justifiable while for the other it is intolerable. At least, the question of national policy priorities must be raised in considering the topic of coercion.

The psychological dimension of liberalization involves the fact that the coercion, threats, and intimidation Azrael points to exist only in the perception of the individual. The core question is whether the Soviet citizen himself perceives an increase or a decrease in official coercion of his own behavior. The absence of adequate survey data on this question makes a fair judgment difficult. Strenuous resistance to state censorship policies by some artists and writers, reported recently in the Soviet press, suggests to Azrael that there is a deep sense of unwarranted restrictions in the arts. But when Azrael contends that the public organizations represent an intensification of coercive control over the behavior of Soviet citizens, Harold Berman takes issue. "The comrades' courts that I have seen in action," Berman reports, "have impressed me by the good spirit with which they act and with which they are received." That the level of coercion, by any definition, is still far higher in the Soviet Union than in most Western countries is indisputable. But whether that level is rising or falling, in the perception of the Russian people, is a question to which only tentative and impressionistic answers can be given.

Equality and Discrimination in Soviet Society

The final group of essays examines four aspects of Soviet life—social, ethnic, religious and intellectual—in which questions of equality and freedom are at issue. The right not to be discriminated against unfairly on the basis of occupation, creed, or nationality has been stipulated above as an essential quality of a liberal society. As the authors in this section make clear, the Soviet record is a poor one in this regard, particularly in the matter of religion. The violent intensification of the anti–religious campaign in the years 1959–64 was aimed at the "final and complete uprooting of religious prejudices" in Soviet society. Likewise, since 1958 the policy of Khrushchev and his successors, as Professor Bilinsky points out, has been to effect a "more pronounced subordination of the interests and aspirations of the individual nationalities to the interests of the Soviet Union and its predominant ethnic group, the Russians."

In both areas of Soviet life, however, there has been some degree of change in government policies during the past few years. In its current policy toward the non–Russian nationalities, the government has made more efforts to ensure Russian control over the major political organs of the state and the republics than to further cultural assimilation and eliminate national differences. Thus Khrushchev's warning to the 22nd Party Congress (1961) that "even the slightest vestige of nationalism should be eradicated with uncompromising Bolshevik determination" has recently been given a narrower, more strictly political, interpretation than in the earlier post–Stalinist period.

In the religious sphere, Bohdan Bociurkiw notes a recent change of mind and mood among those engaged in anti–religious activities. Having for decades indulged in "vulgar misrepresentations of religion, concentration on priestly 'frauds' and 'immorality,' insults to believers, and the widespread reliance on intimidation and coercion in closing churches and dissolving religious congregations," the government has belatedly come to realize that such tactics are self–defeating. "The closing of a parish does not make atheists out of the believers," a Soviet writer points out in Komsomolskaya *Pravda*. "On the contrary, it intensifies the people's attraction towards religion and, in addition, embitters their hearts." Furthermore, the anti–religious campaign has deteriorated because of indifference in the party and Komsomol rank–and–file, and because of widespread lack of support from intellectuals and workers, many of whom feel, as Bociurkiw points out, that religious beliefs do not pose any threat to the regime and, in any case, are "a private matter which must not be held against people in the allocation of jobs and benefits."

In contrast to its discriminatory policies toward religious and ethnic minorities, the government's attitude toward social class relations has been decidedly egalitarian. During the past few years, the party leadership has acted to reduce the privileges and immunities of upper–status, affluent Russians and to increase the well–being and self–respect of workers and peasants. To accomplish this, as Robert Feldmesser indicates, it has raised minimum wages, recruited more peasants into the party, abolished uniforms, ranks, and titles in civilian occupations, and, in general, attempted to "raise the ordinary worker's self–respect and to imbue him with the consciousness—denied him under Stalin—of his own contribution to the country's industrial progress."

Although he praises one aspect of these developments, Feldmesser questions both the motives of the leadership and the long–term effects of such measures. He maintains that the government's attack on the privileges of the elites is really intended to diminish their ability to challenge the party's leadership, and that narrowing the social and economic gaps between the privileged and the unprivileged will ultimately enhance and intensify the party's control over the whole society. Thus, he concludes, "Khrushchev is not repudiating Stalinism; he is, if anything, reinstating it." The issue is a complex one, for on the one hand one might argue, against Feldmesser, that if the means used by the leadership to diminish the status of elites result in a substantial increase in the political participation, well–being, and self–respect of ordinary citizens, the net effect would be a positive gain in the direction of liberalization, no matter how the elites are affected. On the other hand, insofar as interest group elites are coming to fragment the party's power by performing a representative function within the political system, diminishing their status and influence would hamper the growth of a viable pluralism which is also an essential quality of a liberalizing society. In any case, major changes in social relationships are likely to take place grad-

ually and in response to a variety of social and economic forces
rather than as an immediate consequence of the intentions of the
present party leadership.

A similar conclusion seems warranted in the cultural and intellectual sphere of Soviet life. Peter Viereck argues that significant
changes are under way in these areas despite the fact that "there
have been no sweeping changes in Stalinist personnel nor in the
official language and aim of ideological control. . . ." What has
made the impetus toward greater intellectual freedom a compelling one is, to quote Ilya Ehrenburg, "the new knowledge and
strength of the Russian people themselves."

There is in this development no overt challenge to the institution of one-party control over politics and economics, a fact of
life "sincerely accepted by Russia's literary rebels. . . ." Yet the
long-term issue central to the whole subject of liberalization is
whether such cultural momentum will spill over into the political
sphere, and thus threaten Communist Party rule. Viereck believes
this may happen only if the party refuses to accede to the demand for greater cultural and intellectual freedom. Such a development would present the Communist system with a crisis more
serious, perhaps, than any it has faced since the Revolution, but
it is probably too much to expect that the outcome of such a
crisis would be a truly liberal, democratic Russia. At least it seems
reasonably certain that there are major changes under way in
the Soviet system; and that *one* of the possible outcomes is a
gradual evolution back toward the mainstream of Western liberal
development.

Inevitably, domestic changes in the Soviet system are affected
by the dangers and opportunities which the leadership sees in the
international environment. As the leading state in an international
alliance, as well as the psychological center of a world-wide
Marxist movement, the Soviet Union's internal development necessarily accommodates itself, in some measure at least, to an external public of substantial proportions. Nevertheless, this volume
focusses largely on domestic developments, primarily because, despite international ramifications, the major impetus for reform in
the USSR comes from within. The building of "socialism in one
country" is as real and necessary a priority to the present Soviet
leaders as it was to every one of their predecessors. The following
discussions, therefore, are directed primarily to the myth or reality
of liberalization within the Soviet Union.

I

Popular Participation in the Political Process

ROBERT CONQUEST

Soviet Communism: The Antithesis of Democracy

Robert Conquest's accomplishments span several fields. Long noted as a poet and literary critic, he has also written a number of scholarly works as a social scientist. In addition, he has served in the British foreign service. His books on the Soviet Union include Power and Policy in the USSR *(1961) and* Russia After Khrushchev *(1965). He has been a Research Fellow at the London School of Economics and Political Science, and was recently Senior Fellow at Columbia University's Russian Institute.*

IT WOULD BE generally agreed that the Soviet Union is passing through a transitional stage. What the transition is *from* is clear enough, though there may be various views about the other end of the process, set as it is in a not easily determinable future. In any case, we may accept the fact that transitions of this type, although they may later appear to have been comparatively smooth at some basic level, are marked by a great political instability at the top. Even on short-term political moves, as the events of the past ten years in the international Communist movement should perhaps have taught us, we should not expect a smooth and easily predictable development. One may keep an entirely open mind and try to consider the remotest possibilities as carefully as those which appear to be more probable, but it is still only too likely that one will end up saying, as Euripides does at the end of the *Bacchae*: "The things I expected did not come to pass, and the end of the path which I could not discern led to this."

From Robert Conquest, *Russia After Khrushchev* (New York, 1965), pp. 10, 21–27, 29, 31–36. Reprinted by permission of Frederick A. Praeger, Inc.

We cannot "predict" even the immediate Soviet future. But we can examine the nature and tendencies of Soviet politics and of Soviet politicians as they are today, and the various possible results to which the play of these forces may lead.

*   *   *

We have seen that Stalin's rise to power was the occasion for repressions against the humanist element that still remained in Communism. The war mentality was again introduced into the Party by the process of launching it on what might be called the second civil war, in 1929. Not only was the opposition to Stalin crushed outside and inside the Party; even those who supported him merely as the result of political arguments were all executed, to be replaced by those whose devotion was unreasoned. This evolution to ruthlessness and thoughtlessness had its roots. The men who rose to the top were a special selection from the Party's past.

Lenin had constantly complained after the Revolution that Party members were inclined to be insufficiently ruthless, particularly toward their former comrades, the Mensheviks. He put before them the example of the Jacobins (although Engels had powerfully condemned the terror of 1793).

In these circumstances, two things happened: those whose ruthlessness needed no encouragement flourished, and those who had a milder side gradually began to give the violent side of their nature a freer hand. (Those who remained in any degree loyal to humanist theories, even though prepared for temporary violence under the conditions of the Civil War, became the Workers' Opposition and the Democratic Centralists.) But it is worth noting that the effective Stalinists came up for the most part during the late 1920's. Their experience was not simply of *ordering* executions, as Zinoviev and other leaders had done, but of actually carrying them out. They were not in the top circles already as a result of revolutionary work in the underground and in exile. They rose precisely on account of their ruthlessness in the post-Revolutionary period. The Stalinist cadre, which held most of the Party positions by 1930, faced in the collectivization campaign a further test of its ability pitilessly to impose the ruler's will. By now, most of its members doubtless thought nothing about the physical destruction of "class enemies." The kulaks had just been declared such a class. But it must have been obvious that the terror in the countryside actually fell on the peasantry as a whole, and at the same time that the whole policy was quite disastrous from the point of view of the national economy. Those who ran the cities were similarly engaged in imposing backbreaking labor, severe military discipline, and hunger rations on the proletariat itself. At this time, any who had qualms about terror—not against Mensheviks or kulaks, but against the very "people" they were supposed to serve—fell by the wayside.

Yet there was a further test, even for this hardened cadre. Particularly after 1934, they had to turn the same weapons against the actual Party membership, and more often than not against men they knew perfectly well to be innocent in every conceivable sense, even politically. Once again, the process of natural selection drew from the already hard-bitten terrorists of the Party *aktiv* the minority whose enthusiastic fulfillment of the dictator's murderous orders never wavered. It was not simply a question of killing Party members with different views. For it began to involve the Stalinists themselves. The Seventeenth Party Congress, in 1934, was virtually free of opposition representation; but more than half the participants were shot, together with 70 per cent of the Central Committee elected at that time. The new Stalinist promotions to the Politburo went through a similar winnowing. It follows that the survivors were of a highly specialized type. Only three important provincial secretaries lived through the Yezhov terror—Khrushchev, Zhdanov, and Beria. (Meanwhile, the other veterans of an earlier Stalinism were being replaced by a younger generation—those who were to rise to the top in the 1950's and 1960's.) A hypertrophied sort of politician to whom humanist ideas counted for nothing was being bred by a process of natural selection. The struggle for power, which in any political regime must be an exceedingly potent force, became an all-consuming passion.

This bias suited the rule of terrorist bureaucrats rather than politicians proper. In the early days of the Party, and indeed right up to Stalin's attainment of power, prominent Party officials did not play a more important part than that of leading figures in the propaganda or administrative area. The same applied to the industrial and economic managers (for whom a claim to a full share of influence was openly put at the time of the Twelfth Party Congress, in 1923). But Stalin's control of the Secretariat put an end to all that.

Through this he gained control of the supposedly elective bodies of the Party and, through them, of the government apparatus. Finally, he and his private Secretariat formed the center of the State and the party, above and in control of all the organs of power in the country. In the late 1940's he had concentrated most of the power and prestige on the governmental side. Just before his death, however, his preference was again turning to the Party machinery. None of these changes were of any basic importance, though they often reflected changes in policy—since certain machinery was more suitable for the implementation of certain policies; for example, ideological terror (as in 1946–48) was best exercised through the Party. In fact, there were occasional reorganizations in Stalin's time, but the essence remained the same.

In the same way, changes of detail, sometimes of quite a striking nature, have occurred in the past few years. The leadership exercises its control over the country through a variety of institutions, some Party, some State, and some public. The kinds of reorganization that have taken place—in Stalin's time as well as now—have involved no essential change.

As a case in point, one of the most striking of the 1962 organizational changes was the setting up of a single Committee of State and Party Control under Shelepin.[1] In effect, the control organs have always been part of the police side of Soviet life. That is, they had powers of investigation and, in effect, of dismissal, though not of arrest and punishment. Even without changes of form, their significance and power have varied. For example, for many years the Minister of State Control was Merkulov, a close associate of Beria, and a secret police veteran. This meant that the organ was, in effect, a subsidiary arm of Beria's Ministry of the Interior (MVD) and Ministry of State Security (MGB), the police organs. After Beria's arrest, it was transferred to the charge of a nonentity and became a routine operation. In 1956, during a period of Khrushchev's weakness, Molotov took over. During the following year, as was later complained, he made it an agency for conducting his own inquiries toward discrediting his opponents. (It was even said that it "terrorized" other State organs.)

The 1962 merging of this Ministry with a Party body appears to be a revolutionary move. But from the point of view of the country as a whole, it represents, if anything, simply a strengthening, an improvement of efficiency in the ruling organs. Indeed,

[1] This committee was again divided into separate Party and State agencies following Khrushchev's ouster.

the very move points up strikingly the absence of any absolute difference, and any distinction in principle, as apart from convenience, between the apparatuses of Party and State.

It is sometimes implied that the transfer of duties from the State to the Party apparatus, or vice versa, may be a sign of democratic progress. Why this should be thought is hard to understand. For whichever organ passes down the decisions, the decisions themselves are those of the ruling oligarchy, under whose control *all* the various apparatuses come. (Changes of this sort may have political significance in indicating changes in the balance of power between sections of the apparatus, but that is a very different point.)

Administrative and economic difficulties that have beset Russia over the past decade have led to all sorts of such experiments in the organization of the ruling machine. But there has never been any concession of power to the ruled. The rider is riding his horse less brutally, with less use of spurs and whip, but he is still in the saddle.

It has sometimes been suggested that the occasional experiments (as in 1957) with granting greater local initiative to local authorities represent in some way an extension of democracy. But on examination one finds that these were always completely compatible with the principle of dictatorship. The comparison to be made is with an army. In World War II, the high commands of all armies granted, in fact insisted on, much greater tactical responsibility in lower formations than in World War I. Many more decisions on local matters had to be taken by platoon, company, battalion commanders, and so on. But this in no way meant that they were less disciplined, less restricted to the carrying out of the intentions of the commanding generals than before. Nor, if it comes to that, were they any less "militaristic" for such reasons. In this, as in many other ways, the Soviet Communist Party is quite comparable to an army.

Russia (and, following it, all the other Communist countries to varying degrees) has been for decades and still is ruled by professionals of the political machine in a way that has not been the case in any other form of state. The closest parallel description from the West of what political life is like in Russia is to be found in James Farley's *Behind the Ballots*. Farley gives a brilliant account of how what the Americans call ward politics is conducted in the big cities of the United States. He shows how the controllers of the city machine prevent ambitious local leaders from becoming too powerful by raising up against them "rank and file" revolts in their own wards, and in general the techniques that are bound to prevail in such organizations. The difference is that in America the type of thing Farley describes is only a part and not the decisive part of political life: the De Sapios do not rise to the Presidency, and it is rare that any but the lowest courts and the most local of law-enforcement authorities are in the hands of the machine. So that, in general, the struggle cannot be conducted in the uninhibited fashion that the more extreme political toughs would perhaps like. If we imagine a super-Tammany, given a political monopoly and provided with full control of the press, the police, and the courts over the entire area of the United States, we may begin to envisage *something* of the Soviet situation.

As a basic reality, the Soviet polity consists of three elements: (1) a ruling oligarchy of *apparatchiks* and (2) a bureaucratic machine for transmitting its orders to (3) the population. Every organization in the U.S.S.R., operating in every area of life, is in principle, to use the Communists' own expression, a "transmission belt" for Party policy.

Certain changes have been made in the actual machinery of transmission. And orders and decisions are not enforced with the same brutality. But the basic principle remains today what it was under Stalin. The trade unions are, overtly, a means of controlling the workers. The autonomous regions and republics represent a method of controlling the minorities. And so on.

As to the size of this *pays légal* of the Soviet Union, although the various sources are not in complete agreement, they are adequate to yield the round number that is all we require. These show that if, as seems most realistic, we limit ourselves to the bureaus of the provincial committees and higher organs (including candidate members), there are about 2,600 men involved. To these must be added a good many Party workers in the Army and elsewhere, but if we doubled the figure we would be making a liberal estimate. Between 5,000 and 6,000 thus seems the limit of real participants in political life in the U.S.S.R. There are in addition about 8,000 Party workers who are attached in a professional capacity to these bureaus and doubtless have some minimal influence. If we are to count the full membership of provincial committees, we get a figure of about 20,000, and again doubling this for reasons similar to those given above, we may talk of 40,000 being in some way involved in political discussion around the extreme periphery of power.

It is also important to understand the continuity not merely of institutions, but also of personnel from the Stalin epoch to to-day. . . . There are among the present Central Committee members and candidates twenty who were in it as constituted in 1939–41. There are forty-two men who were members of Stalin's 1952 Central Committee, and six who were candidate-members of it. Six full members of the present Presidium (out of ten) and two candidate-members (out of six) were among those forty-two. . . . In fact (and the same applies all the way down the line), every one of the present leadership, and all the subordinates of any significance at all, held posts of trust, higher or lower, in the Stalinist political machinery. And, in general, the youngest group of all were just entering the dictator's service in the particularly bad years preceding his death.

Thus, the leading personnel of the present regime are the product of the Stalin era, just as its institutions are. To make this clear is not by any means to imply that all progress is impossible under the Soviet system as it now exists. Improvements, and important ones, have taken place. But they are neither complete nor irreversible. If we consider them soberly, we shall be able to distinguish between what has been done and anything resembling a genuine democratization.

The present regime in Russia is *sui generis*. But we can usefully define it in terms not so dissimilar to those used for certain other types of rule in the past. On the one hand, it is a bureaucracy of a special kind that could be particularized as "apparatocracy." On the other hand, it has its theoretical justifications, to a degree previously seen only in regimes thought of as theocratic. Theocratic is obviously an unsuitable description, but it will not confuse us if we think of the U.S.S.R. as an ideocratic apparatocracy.

It might be thought that a ruling group with such a background is an unlikely instrument for the "liberalization" of the U.S.S.R. which is now so much spoken of. The possibility indeed exists that, over the long term, democracy, the rule of law, and the end of centralized, all-pervading, self-perpetuating oligarchy may be in store for Russia. But the idea that these sweeping changes are likely to be achieved by the efforts, or at the desire, of any faction within the present ruling hierarchy is another matter. And still less sense can be made of current assertions that something of the sort is already taking place.

A good deal of confusion results from the indiscriminate use of the word "liberal" with regard to Communist (and particularly

Soviet) politics. We must here make an important—indeed, an absolutely basic—distinction. When it is said that the present system of rule in Russia is more "liberal" than Stalin's, this is perfectly true in one sense: the population is far better treated. Arbitrary arrest is now the exception rather than the rule. And, in general, the consumer, the minorities, the writers, the peasants are all subject to less stringent regimentation. But to equate this with anything approaching democratization is completely erroneous. They are still subject to regimentation.

Even within the Party, there have been only very slight signs of a devolution of authority, certainly going no further than the provincial committees. The effective elite may thus have expanded from a dozen to a hundred people, or perhaps even a couple of thousand. This, however, is not an increase in democracy, but merely an expansion of oligarchy. The enlargement of the Roman ruling circle from the few scores in the Senate to the thousands in the Praetorian Guard brought no democratic advantage.

To seek and expect any significant changes from the present rulers of the Soviet Union is to be unjustifiably sanguine. H. G. Wells, dealing with a future oligarchical society in which a leader has made use of popular pressures to oust his immediate rivals, has one of his characters express such hopes:

"But there has been a revolution," he said. "All these things will be changed. Ostrog. . ."
"That is our hope. That is the hope of the world. But Ostrog will not do it. He is a politician. To him it seems things must be like this. He does not mind. He takes it for granted. . . ."

Meanwhile, we may consider the central problem of true liberalization. As one observer commented when the current relaxations were mentioned, "Yes, but what about yesterday—and tomorrow?" All the "liberalizing" steps depend on the will of the leadership and can (in principle, at any rate) be retracted. In the past few years, there have been periods of tough reaction on cultural and other "fronts," and although these have never led to action on a Stalinist scale, the atmosphere of threats and pressures in, for example, 1957 and the first quarter of 1963 was enough to remind one forcibly that there are no guarantees.

Yet we find the London *Observer* flatly asserting: "Under Khrushchev, a start has been made on dismantling the machinery of dictatorship by the regime itself—an almost unprecedented event in history." No facts whatever support this statement. The horrors of Stalin's regime were such that anything less bad must seem, and actually be, a great and welcome improvement. But if Khrushchev's Russia or the Russia of his successors were judged by any standards operating before the rise of Hitler and Stalin, it would be considered an oppressive dictatorship. Even now, if political justifications and partisanships are put aside, one must judge it very much more oppressive than the dictatorships of Salazar or Franco or Tito—although it is true that, disregarding China, there are several regimes in Eastern Europe that are less liberal still.

Nevertheless, it can be argued that it is the direction in which a regime is evolving that counts. Going from worse to bad, it is felt, may be a vector pointing toward good. And Western journalists and visitors, particularly those with some experience of the U.S.S.R. of earlier times, are quick to remark on the improvements. The new Soviet image of Khrushchev's time, which has carried over into the post-Khrushchev era, is the product of such reports, inadequately related to their background and strengthened by the dynamic and purposeful tone of the speeches and "plans." At the same time, the dramatic exposure of parts of the foul Soviet past that were not wholly known before is combined with the hint that there are still forces of darkness abroad that would like to restore such a regime—a "Brand X" that makes the present rulers shine by comparison.

The question to be considered is how far the post-Khrushchevite reformers are willing to go toward really satisfying the inchoate aspirations of the Soviet public. We can perhaps arrive at the probable answer by asking how far they have gone already. First of all, it may be worth listing the areas in which the "permanent" characteristics of Stalinism remain in evidence:

(1) Most important, a self-perpetuating Party bureaucracy remains completely in charge. No sharing whatever of its power with any other part of the population has taken place.

(2) The peasant, in spite of improvements in terms of tenure, continues to be a collectivized serf.

(3) The trade unions remain, in practice, simply adjuncts of the Party and governmental machine. Wage decisions are still imposed on the worker.

(4) The consumer, though to a lesser degree than formerly, still has to put up with low standards because of the channeling into

capital goods and defense products of a proportion of the national income far higher than he would freely grant.

(5) "Socialist realism" remains the official law of the arts. Truly heterodox work is still banned.

(6) Control of all organs of information remains a Party monopoly. Even foreign books are admitted only as selected by cultural bureaucrats.

(7) The minority nationalities continue to live under strictly centralized control from Moscow. Great purges, carried out in reprisal against an extremely mild degree of nationalism, have swept away the party leaderships of republics from Latvia to Azerbaidzhan and Central Asia; the influx of Russians has led to the virtual partition of Kazakhstan.

(8) Travel abroad is permitted only to a limited number of citizens.

(9) The labor camp network, though much shrunken since Stalin's time, continues to function. The laws against political opposition remain draconic.

(10) Soviet political history, including the record of collectivization and the purges, is still taught in an entirely false and misleading fashion. So is foreign history.

A formidable list! And what can be set against it? That all the same basic policies were imposed in a more intolerable and rigid fashion under Stalin.

For someone who has been chastised with scorpions for any length of time, it is no doubt quite a relief to have the chastiser go back to whips again. And it would be quite false to ignore the change for the better in Soviet conditions. Yet a double objection still remains. First, whips are unpleasant enough. Second—and in some ways a more cogent objection—Soviet society remains divided into the whippers and the whipped, and the whippers retain the right to decide what form the relationship between the two shall take in the future.

In so far as the new image of the Soviet Union obscures these facts, it is a dangerous mirage. We may welcome the improvements already made and we may hope for new ones, but to delude ourselves serves no useful purpose whatsoever.

T. H. RIGBY

The Democratic Impulse in the Communist Party

T. H. Rigby is a Professorial Fellow in Political Science at the Institute of Advanced Studies, Australian National University. He has served as Secretary to the British Embassy in Moscow and as Visiting Professor at the Russian Institute at Columbia University. Professor Rigby is the editor of Stalin *(1966) and co-editor of* The Disintegrating Monolith: Pluralist Trends in International Communism *(1965), as well as the author of numerous articles on Soviet political affairs.*

THE RULES AND PROCEDURES governing Party elections which were introduced in the late 1930's have changed very little in subsequent years. They have provided a workable formula for maintaining effective apparatus control over Party appointments and the membership of Party executive and representative bodies, while creating a more convincing impression of "intra-Party democracy" than previously. This impression has rested heavily on a notion of democracy which carries much further the tendency noted earlier to stress participation rather than choice. The whole election process is presented as a device to enable rank-and-file members or conference delegates to arrive collectively at "correct" decisions on staffing questions. "Criticism and self-criticism" provide the basis for unanimous judgments about individuals by measuring their performance against "objective" criteria prescribed by higher Party instances. Senior officials are supposed to "guide" this process (who, if not them?), but since it is human to err, the secret ballot is there to guard against "mistakes."

The western observer, unimpressed by the mystique of participatory democracy, may easily be led by the surface display of unanimity to overestimate the extent of bureaucratic control from above and underestimate the degree of local say in the staffing of Party committees. The impression conveyed by a careful reading of official materials published over the last twenty-five years, however, suggests

From T. H. Rigby, "Party Elections in the CPSU," *Political Quarterly* (October/December, 1964), pp. 420–443. Reprinted by permission of the *Political Quarterly* and of the author.

rather a considerable spread of responsibility and quite extensive consultation in the selection of committee members.

Some of the key officials are certainly chosen by higher Party bodies, but the local apparatus has the initiative in proposing other names, and many of their nominations are vested with local government or other organizations or with subordinate Party bodies, if they are not actually suggested by them. It is true, of course, that this process is kept within official circles and is not normally subject to public scrutiny. . . .

After Stalin

After Stalin's death there seems to have been very little change in electoral practices for a year or so. It was only in 1955 that definite signs appeared of a gentle easing of bureaucratic controls and encouragement of a degree of spontaneous participation by the rank and file. . . .

This encouragement of an element of spontaneity in Party elections, at least at the lowest level of the hierarchy, was given a sharp impetus in 1956 by the reaction against the "excesses" of the Stalin era, set in train by Khrushchev's "secret" report to the Twentieth Party Congress. In the elections at the end of 1956 and the beginning of 1957, the readiness of rank-and-file members and delegates to resist regimentation and to insist on having their say reached a point unknown since the 1920's. The reaction of the Central Committee was interesting. At first it continued to denounce officials who violated the election rules to ensure the election of official nominees, and to applaud those Party members who stood out against such "violations." This attitude changed immediately and radically after the "October days" in Poland and Hungary. In December 1956 and January 1957 the elections of raion, city, and oblast [regional] committees took place in an atmosphere far less sympathetic to "spontaneity" than that prevailing during the primary Party organization elections three months earlier. The situation, perhaps, was too explosive to permit of a sudden return to the ways of 1949–53, even if that had been desired by the leadership. But Party publications ceased condoning cases of rank-and-file rejection of official candidates, implicitly restricted the proper role of "criticism from below" to condemning officials already marked for replacement and to administering warnings to slack or complacent officials, and began to represent as dangerous cranks delegates who sought to go beyond these limits in their opposition to official nominees.

Pravda reported a particularly interesting case at a rural raion conference. One of the delegates, not content with the dose of "criticism and self-criticism" administered to the local leaders, "attempted under the guise of criticism to slander the raion Party secretaries and to defame leading officials wholesale." He asserted that the local secretaries ought to be got rid of—they had been imposed on the raion by the oblast leadership, simply because the latter could rely on their unquestioning obedience. The disaffected delegate, a technician employed by the district soviet, was pictured in the report as a "crackpot," banging on the table and hurling abuse, and even maligning Khrushchev's policy of fostering maize production, which he said "is forced on us from above." The delegates, we are assured, were not led astray by this demagogic oratory.

However distorted *Pravda's* account of this incident may be, it apparently describes an attempt to marshal rank-and-file support at a raion Party conference, in order to effect a change in the local leadership against the will of the regional committee. This can hardly have been an isolated case: it would scarcely have been featured in the "Party Life" section of the Central Committee's most widely circulated publication unless it typified a tendency causing serious concern to the Party leadership. It seems clear that the "spontaneity" which had been cultivated at the base of the Party hierarchy over the previous two years had now moved too far and too fast. In the sensitive atmosphere engendered by the Hungarian and Polish crises, the leadership now saw fit to retreat to more secure positions. . . .

All the same, it would be wrong to conclude that the wheel had turned full circle, for although the old techniques for organizing Party elections had been restored in their former vigour, they were now applied in a sociopolitical context which had changed in several important respects. First of all, the sharp decline in the role of police terror had greatly moderated the sanctions applicable to lesser degrees of nonconformity and insubordination. Secondly, the CPSU possessed a far better-educated and better-informed membership in the early nineteen sixties than it had ten years earlier. This was not only a matter of formal schooling. Due to a substantial easing of the censorship and a reduction of distortion and falsification in domestic propaganda, the more intelligent and open-minded Party members now had access to a far wider range of facts about both their own country and the outside world. Moreover, the ferment of 1956, which gave thousands of

Soviet citizens, inside the Party and out, a taste of relative freedom of expression, had provided invaluable lessons in the implications as well as the limits of such freedom under Soviet conditions.

What long-term influence this changed setting will have upon the character of "intra-Party democracy" it is too early to say. For the present, one change appears to be an increase in the amount of informal consultation before the candidates for elective Party office are chosen. . . . A second feature of the current period is that delegates to Party conferences, although more hesitant than in 1956–57 to oppose official nominees openly, appear to be less inhibited than under Stalin in employing indirect measures to express their own preferences. The apparatus, no longer able to rely on bullying as much as in the past, appears to be resorting to closer organizational control to meet this situation and to ensure the smooth election of officially favoured delegates. . . .

Autocracy and Democracy

In focussing its discussion of Soviet Communist Party elections on the tension between autocratic and democratic elements in the Party tradition, and on the manifestation and resolution of this tension during the main phases of the Party's history, the present article has adopted an approach rather at variance with that found in most non-Communist discussions of the subject. There is a fairly general tendency, in stressing the bureaucratic nature of intra-Party relationships, to treat the democratic forms and language as *simply* a propaganda facade. The picture presented here tends to confirm the view that the choice of formally elected officials is in large part the result of bureaucratic processes, but it also suggests that the democratic forms and language are not politically irrelevant. This is a dimension of Soviet political life which has been little explored by Western political scientists.

Why do the Soviet leaders retain this vestigial element of democracy? It was suggested earlier that they may value the rank-and-file veto as a check—one check among several—against seriously inefficient, dishonest, or unpopular officials, particularly at the base of the Party apparatus. But perhaps this is not their only motive. One must remember that the vast majority of Party members never come in direct contact with "intra-Party democracy" at levels higher than the primary Party organization at their place of work. Their attitude to the assumptions underlying the notion of "democratic centralism" will therefore be determined very largely by their experience of it in their own organization. If it can be assumed that the leadership desires them really to accept these assumptions and not just cynically pay lip-service to them, one can see how important it is to retain some semblance of democratic participation by ordinary members at this basic level, some suggestion that the rank-and-file Communists have "the last word."

Any discussion of how Soviet "democratic centralism" appears from the inside is bound to be highly speculative, but when evidence is lacking it is sometimes worth speculating. It seems likely that the majority of Party members take the "democratic" part seriously, and, while aware of the "limitations" in practice, tend to accept these limitations as a temporary necessity. It is possible that many Soviet Communists take something of this attitude with them as they rise to positions of power and authority in the hierarchy. As was noted earlier, although democracy has never been elevated to an absolute good in Leninist doctrine, it is constantly treated as something desirable in itself, to be enjoyed to the fullest extent compatible with the interests of "the revolution." This is one of the many European humanist values which have not been wholly smothered under the blanket of Soviet bureaucracy, and one which receives constant nourishment from the democratic forms themselves and from their incessant propaganda gloss—however tenuous the reality behind these forms may be.

While the history of Party elections lends little support to the view that the Soviet system must necessarily become more democratic as the U.S.S.R. "matures," grows richer, and better educated, the viability of the democratic ideal even under very unfavorable conditions is indicated by the way these forms tend to take on substance whenever circumstances are favorable. The most recent illustration of this was the activation of "intra-Party democracy" in the de-Stalinization era of 1956–57.

At present, the tension between autocratic and democratic elements in the Communist tradition shows few signs either of disappearing or of growing to dimensions which might threaten the stability of the Soviet regime. Of course, there is no assurance that some future era of reforms or succession struggle will not exacerbate this tension to an unheard-of pitch of intensity. Since the internal and international environments are constantly changing, the past history of the CPSU affords no sure guide as to how such a crisis would be resolved.

WILLIAM M. MANDEL

The Emergence of Democracy in Post-Stalinist Russia

William M. Mandel is a specialist on the USSR and translator of Soviet social science works into English. He is the author of The Soviet Far East and Central Asia: A Guide to the Soviet Union, Russia Re-Examined, *and numerous articles. He has been a post-doctoral Fellow in a Slavic Studies program at the Hoover Institution at Stanford University and is a former Research Associate of the American Russian Institute of New York. Professor Mandel is currently teaching in the Sociology Department at San Francisco State College. His extensive travel in the Soviet Union includes one visit of a year's duration.*

ALTHOUGH THE U.S.S.R. is not remotely civil libertarian, there is a vast amount of participatory democracy on many vital subjects, when the decision is made to open them to public discussion. I have already mentioned the breadth of the "Libermanism" discussion. The psychology of Soviet citizens consequently reflects the assumption that government must listen to the people. I have numerous tapes carrying the tone of the nineteen-year-old lounging by the Moscow River who said to me in 1966: "You've *got* to send a message to the President that the American people doesn't want that war in Vietnam . . . he has *got* to listen to you, to the voices of his electors." A woman commented on a similar remark in another discussion: "But the people don't decide much [in America]. Their democracy, in general, isn't as effective as it is with us. For all practical purposes there is no democracy." When I commented that most Americans thought the shoe on the other foot, and cited the differences in elections, a barrage of responses from the crowd offered what the speakers regarded as proofs of the democracy of their elections. They all knew the names of their

From "Toward a More Humane and Equal Society," by William M. Mandel, in Samuel Hendel and Randolph L. Braham, *The USSR After 50 Years* (1967), pp. 181–187. Reprinted by permission of Alfred A. Knopf, Inc.

"congressmen," unlike the experience of the Stanford student (reporting in the *San Francisco Chronicle,* August 14, 1966), that "none of the people I talked to on the streets [of a ghetto in Brooklyn] had any idea who his congressman was."

In 1965 and 1966, a national discussion occurred to frame new model rules for collective farms to replace the existing set, thirty years old. The discussion was carried on for many months in the 5 million daily-circulation national newspaper read by the peasantry, *Sel'skaia zhizn'* (Rural Life), which published in detail a vast variety of notions coming from the grass roots. In November 1965 the U.S.S.R. Academy of Sciences' Institute of State and Law convened a conference on the subject. Its participants were people from research institutes and higher educational institutions in law, economics, and agriculture, the agriculture ministries of the U.S.S.R. and of its Russian republic, the Moscow Regional Farm Administration, the U.S.S.R. and Russian Republic "attorney-generals' " offices (procuracies), publishing houses, newspaper and magazine editorial boards. Although a majority of persons at such a gathering would certainly be members of the Party, hardly anyone mentioned that organization, and no one deferred to the official rank or the structure represented by any other speaker.

Speakers whom one might expect to seek to protect the rights of bureaucracy took precisely the opposite position. The opening speaker, a legal scholar, had proposed that the model rules have the force of law. But then a representative of the U.S.S.R. Agriculture Ministry's Division of Collective Farms held that that would deprive the farmers of the right to change or amend them. An academician with a distinctly Central Asian name, Shaibekov, from the University of Kazakhstan, informed the body that his republic had not waited for a lead from the federal level but had drafted its own proposed model rules, which he urged be considered for the U.S.S.R. as a whole. He protested the tendency, more marked in Kazakhstan than elsewhere because of the vast virgin-soil planting program, to reorganize collective (cooperative) farms into state (government-owned) farms without their consent, and wanted the model rules to specify that the government of the given republic must give its approval. (The Party Congress subsequently fell in line, with a policy of drastically curtailing such reorganizations.)

A federal government spokesman urged that the size of the collective farmer's private plot and the number of livestock he could possess individually be tied to his contribution of work in the collective itself. But, the Soviet law journal[1] reporting this meeting said, "A majority of the participants in the conference held otherwise."

There was sharp difference of opinion over town meeting versus representative democracy in governing the farms. Some held that no farm should be permitted to be so large that all its members could not gather in the local rural hall to decide fundamental problems. A speaker who had formerly chaired a 72,000-acre farm cited his experience in favor of representative democracy. The discussion showed the actual level of attendance at general farm meetings to be extraordinarily high by the standards of membership organizations in the West. Three hundred out of eighteen hundred was regarded as an example of an unacceptably small gathering, not even comprising a legal quorum empowered to do business. (Four percent of membership is normal at trade union meetings in the United States. The most controversial meeting in the history of the Berkeley, California Consumers Co-op brought out two percent of its 40,000 members in this highly-educated and turbulent community.)

In view of my discussion of the future of the Party, it is exceptionally significant that some speakers emphasized that only a member of the given collective farm should be eligible to be its manager. Hitherto, it had been the Party's practice to send outsiders in, in much the same way as the head of a state farm is named by the superior agency.

A speaker noted that while the work of collective-farm management, professional people (veterinarians, etc.) working on the farms, and equipment operators was guaranteed remuneration by government legislation, the rank-and-file collective farmer had no such protection, and was entirely dependent upon the crop and other products. The Party Congress a few months later committed itself to the institution of a guaranteed wage for farmers during the current Five Year Plan. In May 1966, the Party and government *recommended* to the collective farms that they pursue this policy as of July 1 of that year. The fact that this carried no force beyond recommendation to economically independent entities is evidenced by the publication of reports nine months later that there were still farms not paying a guaranteed wage.

[1]The conference report appeared in *Sovetskoe gosudarstvo i pravo,* No. 3 (1966), unabridged translation in *Soviet Law and Government* (White Plains, New York: International Arts and Sciences Press, Summer, 1966).

As this book went to press, the new model rules had not yet been adopted. It may be speculated that the extraordinary advance of agriculture in 1966 strengthened the hand of those who wished to leave well enough alone. But the nature, form, and extent of the discussion makes clear that the situation with respect to the rules does represent the consensus of Soviet opinion, very much including the rank-and-file.

To regard democracy as inseparable from confrontation of opposing candidates on election day is hardly sustained by the experience of the West. The *Los Angeles Daily Journal*, a newspaper for lawyers in our second largest metropolitan area, carried in 1965 an advertisement by Hal Evry stating: "Leading public relations firm with top-flight experience in statewide campaign wants attorney general candidate." A reporter's inquiry in the *San Francisco Chronicle* (December 3, 1965) brought the following comment from Mr. Evry: "People are generally unsophisticated. The issues just confuse them. The best way to manipulate them is with a simple slogan they can understand. And it's better *if they never see the candidate.*" (My emphasis.) Mr. Evry managed the successful race in 1958 for congressional candidate George Kasem, a Democrat who won in a district that had previously been Republican territory.

Misuse of the system of competitive elections by the power of the campaign fund shrewdly employed does not mean the system should be junked, but neither does it justify its use as an absolute criterion of democracy. In 1966, for the first time in thirty years, a responsible Soviet political figure proposed that the U.S.S.R. make use of competitive elections. Mr. N. K. Arutiunian, former rector of the University of Armenia and head of state of that Soviet republic at the time of his speech, said to the congress of the Armenian Communist Party:

It has always been argued that where there are no antagonistic classes, it makes no sense to put up two or more candidates since this would lead to futile rivalry and opposition. . . . Unity does not mean a complete homogeneity of all the opinions and feelings of the people, of their talents and energies, their methods of work and public activity. . . . The nomination of more than one candidate . . . would . . . increase their [the voters'] political activity and interest, would raise the level of responsibility of the candidates toward their electors (*The N.Y. Times,* March 22, 1966).

Support for the idea at least reached a level at which *Izvestia* found it necessary to devote a lengthy article (May 13, 1966) to defense of the one-candidate system. (My own probings that summer did not indicate this to be a live issue among the people, who indicated vocal satisfaction with the present system under which several candidates are named informally and only one appears on the ballot after discussion at meetings.)

The sense of realism that emerges from Mr. Arutiunian's speech, as from the collective-farm rules discussion, reaches into most realms of Soviet life and suggests future trends. For example, the notion that unemployment is simply impossible in a socialist country (except for people who are merely between jobs) has been discarded in favor of the understanding that socialism eliminates its causes but that there may be unemployed unless planning properly distributes industry geographically to the places where population factors have produced an unused labor supply. This knowledge itself is a result of the freedom for sociological research that has developed in the past decade. Given this information, the control over the economy provided by public ownership can be brought into play. In February 1966, a joint resolution of Party and government made provision for schooling and jobs for the extraordinary 70 percent increase in eighteen-year-olds in the two preceding years reflecting the sudden demobilization of the army after World War II. One of its provisions will suffice to illustrate its association with the socialist nature of the economy. All managements were ordered, depending upon the employment problem and skill levels required, to save 5 percent to 10 percent of *total* places on the payroll, as instructed by *local* authorities, for youth newly entering the labor market, with an even higher percentage permissible for 1966 alone, when a school reform put two graduating classes on the labor market simultaneously.

Another example of the unfreezing of attitudes is presented in an article by Yu. Kariakin, a social critic, originally appearing in the *World Marxist Review,* from which it was picked up by *Novy Mir.* The article is in support of Alexander Solzhenitsyn's novel of life in Stalin's concentration camps, *One Day in the Life of Ivan Denisovich.* Those who attack that novel (and one speaker did so at the Twenty-third Party Congress, four years after publication), says Kariakin with bitterness, uphold "the communism of the barracks." He quotes Mao Tse-tung as having written: "Real love of man is possible, but only after classes have been abolished everywhere in the world." To which Kariakin responds:

The principles of communist humanism must be brought to reality not only in a remote future, but today; *otherwise they will never be.* If they are not observed day in and day out, they will be postponed to eternity. What is most important is that these principles be cultivated from *earliest* childhood. And if we inoculate all children against a number of diseases, and do so successfully, it is all the more important to protect people from *childhood* against the psychology that rules in the "city of identical little men," which unfortunately exists not only in the fairy tale. [My emphasis.]

And he finds a line in one of Lenin's last articles that is a cry for individual dignity: "Lenin said that the destiny of Russia, the fate of the revolution, depended upon those 'of whom one can swear that they will take no word on faith, say no word against conscience.' "[2]

The stand taken by Solzhenitsyn and Kariakin is that widely accepted by thinking Soviet youth today. A literary critic reviewing Yevtushenko's *Bratsk Hydroelectric Station* for the middle-of-the-road magazine *Znamia* says: "The organizing idea of his poem is contained in the words, 'we are not slaves,' and in irreconcilability to all forms of slavery, physical and intellectual, and whether their second form makes the fact of slavery evident, or whether it conceals them. . . ." The critic adds:

The unifying principle in *Bratsk Hydroelectric Station* is rather the spirit of the ethics of citizenship. Today we perceive acutely that the further development and destiny of the revolution and, consequently, of human history are indissolubly tied to the problem of the moral level of society and consequently to the moral improvement of each individual.[3]

Note that morality is tied to the ethics of citizenship, which in the West we spell out under the concept of democratic values. We have seen the call for competitive elections by the academic and political figure Arutiunian. But it is Kariakin who details in this same article the values in which he believes by attacking those he opposes:

If someone holds that somebody else doesn't have the right to his own convictions, and the latter is ashamed of his opinion, is afraid to express it and tries to get rid of it (meaning he has blind faith in some-

one), you have the basic prerequisite for worship of an individual. . . .
The champions of worship of an individual want to see everything regu-
lated, but in practice they merely give free reign to lawlessness. . . . The
hatred borne him [reference here is to the main character of Solzhenitsyn's
novel] by the present defenders of worship of an individual has a
social origin. Their attitude toward him is such precisely because he has
begun to put questions dangerous for them. . . .

These, then, are Kariakin's democratic values, and those of
the editors of *Novy Mir:* the right to individual opinion, the
courage to express it, the rule of law, free thought, the right to
put questions dangerous to those in positions of authority, a
political party expressing the perceptions of the people. They
clearly believe this possible within the framework of continued
leadership by a reformed Communist Party. And Kariakin asserts
with no less vigor his belief that these values can truly exist for
all only in a society in which the power of private wealth does
not render the freedoms of the majority impotent in practice.
(But these views are held in a society that at present writing still
occasionally jails writers; often delays publication by other writers;
controls the staging of controversial plays and films; limits showings
of avant-garde art; tightly controls foreign travel by its citizens;
continues to ban dissent in the mass media over foreign policy,
Trotsky, drugs and sex deviation; and which limits cultural
expression and education in Yiddish. It is also a society that in
fifteen short years has advanced from holding hundreds of
thousands in forced-labor camps to a situation in which there are
hardly a dozen persons detained for reasons of dissent, this change
having been accomplished under the same political party and without
violence. I know of no comparable *rate* of *nonviolent* progress in
the history of human political institutions.)

II The New Elites and the Development of Pluralism

ALLEN KASSOF

Totalitarianism Without Terror

Allen Kassof is Associate Professor of Sociology at Princeton University. He is a frequent contributor to scholarly journals on Soviet affairs and author of The Soviet Youth Program (*1965*).

MORE THAN A DECADE after Stalin's death, the time is ripe for a fresh view of Soviet society. Many of the conventional patterns of analysis, developed largely during the period of Stalinist absolutism, seem to be no longer adequate for this purpose. This article proposes that a new concept, the "administered society," may be useful in summarizing and evaluating recent changes in the Soviet system and in identifying current trends.

Like other ideal-typical concepts, that of the administered society by no means pretends to account for all of the concrete detail of a social order. Instead, it draws attention (through emphasis, and hence a certain exaggeration) to very general features which constitute a society's ethos or prevailing themes—in the Soviet case, centering around the drive of the regime to establish a highly organized and totally coordinated society, and the consequences of that drive.

The administered society can be defined as one in which an entrenched and extraordinarily powerful ruling group lays claim to ultimate and exclusive scientific knowledge of social and historical laws and is impelled by a belief not only in the practical desirability, but the moral necessity, of planning, direction, and coordination from above in the name of human welfare and progress.

Convinced that there should be complete order and predictability in human affairs, the elite is concerned not merely with

From Allen Kassof, "The Administered Society," *World Politics* (July, 1964), pp. 558–575. Reprinted by permission of *World Politics*.

the "commanding heights," but also to an overwhelming degree with the detailed regulation of the entire range of social life, including those institutions which, in the West, typically have been regarded as lying beyond the legitimate scope of public authority and political intervention. The rulers of the administered society refuse to grant the possibility of unguided coordination and integration; they believe, on the contrary, that not only the masses but responsible subgroups (for example, the professions) are incapable of maintaining a viable social order on their own, without the precise and detailed supervision of an omniscient political directorate. The elite believes, and through a far-reaching program of education and propaganda tries to teach its subjects, that the only possible good society is one that is *administered*.

The administered society is thus a variant of modern totalitarianism, with the important difference that it operates by and large without resort to those elements of gross irrationality (in particular, the large-scale and often self-defeating use of psychological terror and physical coercion as basic means of social control) that we have come to associate with totalitarian systems in recent decades.

The administered society, however, should be distinguished from the conventional welfare state in that it is not involved simply or principally in creating minimal conditions of social welfare within an otherwise pluralistic political framework, but instead treats welfare as an incidental—and instrumental— element in the larger scheme of social planning and reform. While an administered society may display more or fewer welfare features of a material or service nature, they are neither final goals nor the most important determinants of overall policy. To put it another way, the elite regards the promotion of total coordination as itself the ultimate form of welfare under modern conditions.

Plainly enough, the administered society is not the authentic good society of faithful Marxists, for it is characterized by the growing size and importance of an elite party and state bureaucracy, in contrast to the withering-away of governmental apparatus which Marxism predicts and upon which it insists.

Nor, finally, should the administered society be confused with a rational technocracy, even though here there are some superficial parallels. The leadership of the administered society, to be sure, is forced to rely on scientific and technical cadres as sources of essential information and in the execution of highly complex economic and social planning. But the political elite is not bound solely or principally by considerations of technical rationality; the technicians and experts operate only under license of the political elite and in terms of the latter's self-proclaimed ultimate knowledge about the proper uses of science and technology in the larger socio-historical setting. The experts, in short, are servants rather than masters or even independent practitioners. They lack the power of veto on grounds of technical rationality over political decisions (though in the end the limits of technology itself, if not the will of the technocrats, of course impose certain restraints). And their potential for independent influence in the society is decisively cut short by the elite's consistent practice of defining *all* decision-making as political and therefore beyond the competence of any group other than itself. Similar considerations are applied— if anything with more vigor—to the producers of the more "esoteric" goods and services—the artists and writers, professors and critics and journalists. Like technicians in the more literal sense, they are construed by the elite as turning out "commodities" whose creation, distribution, and consumption demand coordination from above in the pursuit of order and planned progress. . . .

SOME EXAMPLES

The case for the administered society is not subject to proof of an absolute kind, for not only is such a concept more or less useful rather than right or wrong, but its application to the affairs of a live society cannot possibly cover all contingencies. It does, however, provide a general framework for depicting the Soviet system under Khrushchev (and probably his successors as well), sensitizing us to interpretations that otherwise might go unnoticed and enabling us to see patterns in apparently unconnected trends. The following examples (at this early stage it would be too much to call them evidence) are chosen from a number of important areas of the Soviet system: . . . administrative shifts in industry and agriculture, the youth program, [and] Khrushchev's position on art and literature. . . .

Controls in Industry and Agriculture

An especially convincing example is to be found in the record of industrial and agricultural organization. Early reaction to the widely publicized administrative reorganizations that gained momentum in the latter half of the 1950's saw in them a kind of decentralization that might lead to the development of an incipient grass-roots autonomy on the local level. The announced desire to improve productive efficiency by granting more discretionary powers to plant and farm managers, it was speculated, also held forth the possibility of autonomies that would go beyond the intended area of purely economic or managerial decision-making; that is, might lead by tiny but cumulative steps to local patriotisms whose long-run effect would be to encourage a modicum of genuine political independence.

The proposition is reasonable enough, for there is a connection between one kind of autonomy and another, even though the actual political consequences of such a situation are necessarily difficult to forecast. However that may be, we now know that the new independence of industrial and agricultural managers has turned out to be largely illusory. As early as 1960, Arcadius Kahan could conclude in a study of agricultural reorganization that the practical consequence of administrative shifts had been to *tighten* Party control by reducing the overweight bureaucratic machine between Moscow and the farm, thereby enhancing the Party's effective presence in local operations. He writes:

The new collective amalgamations, the influx of agricultural specialists and former MTS personnel (often party members) into the farm organizations, along with a drive for new party recruits in rural areas, have made it possible to organize party cells on most collective and state farms. The consequent opportunity to exercise control from within, and to present the party to the mass of peasants as a local rather than an alien force, has undoubtedly increased the party's influence over the behavior of the farm population.

On the industrial side, Herbert Ritvo has made a similar point even more emphatically:

. . . the economic bureaucracy has undergone a series of sweeping reorganizations designed to improve its efficiency and to strengthen direct controls. There can be little doubt that not only the power of leading representatives of this group, but also many of their personal privileges, have diminished as a result of Khrushchev's administrative changes and reforms. As one reads the familiar complaints of industrial managers, it becomes only too apparent how little the "rights of managers" have been expanded since the decree of August 9, 1955. In addition, this sector, more than any other, has felt the greater severity of the new penal laws of 1961–1962; thus, the reorganization of management has revealed that the opinions of this part of the bureaucracy could be silenced and ignored in a matter affecting its vital interests; the harshness of the revised penalties for economic crimes has demonstrated that, despite the importance of the technical elite in an industrial society, their prerogatives are limited—not least by an educational system which can now provide a sufficiency of replacements.

These are not only the conclusions of Western analysts; the fight against the dangers of local autonomy is a matter of high-level policy in the USSR:

. . . from the very beginning Comrade N. S. Khrushchev, to whom belongs the initiative for the reorganization, directed the attention of our economic cadres to the impermissibility of localism in any form and cautioned them against understanding an integrated economy as self-contained and autarchical. Was such a warning necessary? Undoubtedly it was. The relatively small size of many of the economic administrative regions was an objective basis for attempts to develop a self-sufficient economy within the framework of the economic councils.

Both in industry and agriculture, then, the Khrushchev reforms have been liberalizing insofar as they attempt seriously to amend the rigid and inefficient Stalinist pattern of multiple, overlapping, and cross-checking hierarchies between the center and the localities. But at the same time they have given the Party a freer (because more direct and efficient) hand in administering its own interests within the production units. . . .

The Youth Organizations

An additional illustration comes from the Soviet youth organizations. Far from loosening their grip on the new generation in comparison with their practice in Stalin's time, the Komsomol and Pioneers have been involved in intensive efforts to extend their network of influence, both in membership coverage and in the range of youth activities that they originate or supervise. It is true that some steps have been taken to reduce some of the most extreme consequences of excessive bureaucratization and neglect of local interests and, at the most recent Komsomol Congress in 1962, there was some guarded talk about democratizing the internal structure. But a close examination of the recent Komsomol record suggests that the impulse for such changes comes not so much from a serious intention to democratize the youth program as to alter its widespread reputation as boring, repressive, and offensive in order to make it more appealing to youth. At the same time there has been no sign at all of a withdrawal from interference in personal life; if anything, the reforms are meant to make that interference more effective by replacing swivel-chair organizers with energetic enthusiasts who will not be afraid to grapple directly with problems of youthful nonconformity.

Certainly it is true, as in other areas of Soviet life, that the resort to coercion and threat has become less important than under Stalin. But their replacement with more reasoned tactics of persuasion should not be taken as a surrender of the principle of total involvement and control. On the contrary, the youth program is now regarded as more essential than under Stalin, for it has become increasingly important to remind the new generation— which does not share the caution born of experience in the old days—not to confuse the relatively more benign outward character of Khrushchevism with a grant of autonomy. A genuine test of change in the youth sector would be a surrender (more realistically, a partial surrender) of the organizations' claim to a monopoly over formal and informal youth activities. Concretely, such a step might take the form of allowing youngsters (especially in higher educational institutions) not to join if they have no desire to do so. But there has been no change in the Komsomol's policy of covering an ever-larger proportion of those of eligible age, including 100 percent of the university students and large majorities of key categories of young professionals. And the Pioneer organization, as before, continues to maintain total coverage in its group. Finally, the content of the youth program (as revealed in recent policy literature) centers around renewed efforts to exercise total control over the young on the grounds that the reforms now make the organizations such benign and authoritative agencies of society that no one could possibly object to their paternalistic concern.

Literature and Art

In art, literature, and intellectual affairs generally, recent events in the Soviet Union have attracted such intensive scholarly and journalistic coverage in the West that it is hardly necessary to review them here. Most analyses have stressed the alternating thaws and freezes in the intellectual world since Stalin's death, seeking to discern in them an overall trend or to attribute cyclical changes to shifting alignments in the Party leadership or to general characteristics of the political climate.

Granting that the end of this complex story is yet to be told, Khrushchev's now famous speech of March 1963, in which he upbraided errant artists and writers, must stand as a landmark in the publicly proclaimed policy of the administered society. The essence of his message is that the Party's willingness to allow at least some frank discussion of the Stalin period and the decision to loosen somewhat the straitjacket of rigid conformity must not be understood as permission to stray from Party control; that what the more optimistic members of the artistic and intellectual communities have taken for liberalization, or liberation, is only a readjustment in the form and content of Party supervision. In effect, said Khrushchev, either the writers, artists, and others must work out a satisfactory system of self-censorship conforming to the needs of the Party, or the Party will do the censoring itself.

Khrushchev made it clear, then, that artistic and intellectual output is a commodity to be mobilized as the regime sees fit in furthering its domestic and international programs, and that the leeway granted in the process of de-Stalinization has been a measure to improve the quality of the product for these purposes— not a signal that the instrumental approach has been modified or abandoned. The thaws and freezes, that is, have been generated by uncertainty as to how the product could be improved without violating unchanged political requirements. So long as this uncertainty remains, the ups and downs of the artistic and intellectual communities may be expected to continue as the limits of experimentation are redefined in practice. But the basic principle has been reiterated, and unmistakably so. . . .

Some Implications

These illustrations go only a small way towards showing the potential applications of the concept of the administered society to an understanding of contemporary currents in Soviet life. Others, no doubt, would be equally appropriate—for example, the growing emphasis on "public" participation in social control through voluntary assistance to the militia, the Komsomol street patrols' enforcing of dress, decorum, and taste, the quasi-judicial comrades' courts, and so forth.

There are also *a priori* reasons to expect the Soviet leadership to stress this approach. The organizational problems of the Soviet economy, for example, become more rather than less complex with technological advance; if economic successes under Stalin solved a number of relatively primitive problems of accumulation and investment, they in turn have created new problems of organization and coordination that are less easily solved. When Khrushchev rejects the notion that the ship of society can sail wherever the waves carry it, he refers not only to the narrow problem of political unity and ideological correctness but to the larger, underlying issue of how to manage a modern industrial order. In one sense the Soviet case is a qualitatively extreme example of the problem of coordination faced in all modern industrial societies, aggravated by the peculiar ferocity with which the issue of backwardness was handled under Stalin.

The passion for organization, for perfect coordination and integration of social life—a kind of compulsive's dream of beehive order projected upon an entire society—has partly replaced the original impetus of Bolshevik ideology. The denial that there can be any real conflict in the good society, the belief that all legitmate human needs can be satisfied simultaneously, that interest groups are subversive, that only uninformed selfishness or disregard of organizational principles stands between the present and the utopia of the future—these are some of the ingredients of the new ideology. If it lacks some of the romantic appeal of barricade-storming, it is perhaps no less revolutionary in its consequences, for its purveyors insist that they will not rest until all societies have undergone the transformation to superorganization. Its potential impact on an audience, say, of hard-pressed political leaders and court philosophers of developing nations may be considerable, for the idea of total coordination must tempt many of them as the answer to problems and frustrations of economic backwardness and the awkward necessities of coping with competing political interests. And for mentalities especially sensitive to the real and apparent disarray of human affairs or philosophically intolerant of ambiguity in social structure, there is, after all, a great utopian charm in such an image: much like the classical Marxist formula of salvation, it seems to promise a final answer to the centuries-old dislocations generated by modernism and science and a return to a latter-day version of a medieval world where everything—and everyone—apparently had a proper place in the universe.

Assuming this assessment of the basic aspirations of the Soviet regime to be correct, there is the quite different question of how far they are likely to be realized in practice. Naturally it would be unrealistic to expect complete and literal fulfillment of the dream, any more than one could have expected perfect totalitarianism to exist under Stalin. The issue, then, is how closely it will or can be approximated. Without going into the kind of detailed discussion that is far beyond the scope of these early notes, the best that can be done is to suggest some of the factors in a balance sheet of probabilities.

In the background is the ancient dilemma of how to combine personal with public interest in such ways as to put an end to politics. If the record of other complex societies (not to mention the history of the Soviet Union itself) is a guide, we may be excused for having serious doubts about such a grandiose conception. To deny that there is social conflict, as the Soviet leadership essentially does, is not to be rid of it. Even the most superficial reading of the Soviet press daily provides an endless catalogue of the stresses and strains arising from the pursuit of private or group interests against the demands for conformity emanating from the center. Some of the examples are petty, more of them are serious, all of them reflect the underlying tensions of an imperfectly co-ordinated society; they usually fall short of posing immediate threats to the political directorate but often have cumulative consequences of an unplanned and unintended nature. Moreover, broad areas of deviant behavior and subversive attitudes which once were suppressed by the application of prophylactic terror now have to be handled by more patient and indirect means. It is too early to say whether the new machinery of social control will be as adequate to the task as was pure Stalinism.

Then there is the paradoxical discovery, finally dawning on the regime, that the gradual alleviation of extreme material want that has been behind so many traditional problems may produce new and more subtle issues of control over a long-deprived population experiencing relative affluence for the first time. Failures to satisfy these wants are the obvious danger; success breeds more subtle risks, however, for a rising standard of living (as we have seen in the case of other industrial nations) often results in new forms of emotional investment that are to a great extent antithetical to the high level of public commitment obviously essential in realizing the administered society. We already have some evidence of this in the form of a troublesome youth problem in the Soviet Union: one of the greatest headaches of the post-Stalin regime has been how to prevent the drive for individual advancement and the intoxication with consumption from becoming the basis for a privatism that could easily wreck long-term intentions. So far the problem has been most visible among youth, but there is reason to believe that it is widespread.

To these and equally powerful impediments in the road to the administered society—for example, the articulate and sometimes effective objections of at least parts of the scientific, artistic, and intellectual communities to being as totally mobilized as they were under Stalin—must be added the even more vexing "technical" problem of *how* to administer and coordinate an entire enormous society effectively even in the absence of any special opposition. Yet when all this is said, what stands out is the remarkable success of the Soviet regime, during and since Stalin's day, in making a very impressive start.

Most important is the fact that, during almost half a century of Communist rule, the possibilities for alternative institutional forms have been largely wiped out. Even were the will to democratic or pluralistic institutions substantially present—and it is not—it is highly doubtful that the resources currently available by way of formal structures, source philosophies, or practical experience would go very far. The Bolshevization of a society, if it goes on long enough, is an irreversible process, because it is so intense and so total that it indelibly alters not only earlier institutional forms but the entire pattern of a population's expectations of reasonable and workable alternative possibilities for social order. This is not to say that the Soviet leaders have mastered history, for even a process that is irreversible can move forward in unintended and undesired directions. But the prospects of developing viable substitutes for a social system that has so long been based upon extreme and centralized organization are very poor. Ironically, the regime is probably correct—at least in the case of Soviet society—when it insists that any form of pluralism is impossible. The best that can be expected is a more or less benign totalism within the limits of the administered society, with a very slow erosion of the Bolshevik heritage; the worst, a surrender of good intentions to manage the society without terror and a return in some form to the excesses and cruelties of classical Stalinism.

JOSEPH R. STRAYER

The Impetus Toward a Pluralist Society

Joseph R. Strayer is Professor of History and of International Affairs in the Woodrow Wilson School at Princeton University. He is a former Director of the American Council of Learned Societies (1947–51) and a specialist in comparative constitutional history and mediaeval history.

THE "CULT OF PERSONALITY" was denounced by Khrushchev, but his own actions showed that he realized its importance in the Soviet system. The leader must be respected, even if he is not admired; he must appear to be in full control of all important activities, even if in practice he is guided by an inner circle of advisers. Lenin was admired and Stalin was feared, but both achieved full control of the country. Malenkov had too brief a period of authority to make much of an impression and he certainly never had full control. In retrospect, it looks as if Khrushchev was always in a precarious position. He certainly had a vivid personality, but he was never admired enough or feared enough to overcome a rising tide of ridicule and criticism. The present faceless leadership is very much in Malenkov's position and may suffer the same fate. It is always possible that a stimulating and powerful figure, such as Shelepin, will emerge from the present unresolved situation, but even such a man probably will be unable to recapture the prophet's mantle of Lenin or the tyrant's scepter of Stalin. Too many people know that a leader gains his position by intricate political manipulations and not by apostolic succession from Marx and Lenin. With senior party leaders established in strongly entrenched positions it is not easy to override all opposition and criticism. Finally, and most important, Soviet society has become too complex for one man to make and impose decisions in all fields. What is needed is a top-flight manager and coordinator, a man who is as much a politician as a dictator.

Reprinted by special permission from "Problems of Dictatorship; The Russian Experience," *Foreign Affairs* (January, 1966), pp. 267–274. Copyright by the Council on Foreign Relations, Inc., New York.

In fact, the very success of the Communist effort to modernize Russia has created a new political climate. Large groups of experts have emerged—administrators, economic managers, scientists, military leaders—and the opinions of these groups cannot wholly be disregarded. Each group has its own interests to protect; each group believes, often with reason, that it knows better how to solve its own problems than does the top leadership. Each group not only includes many party members, but also has access to and support from men who rank well up in the party hierarchy. The result is that too many people are involved in basic policy decisions to continue the practice of settling all important issues in small secret meetings. There has been an increasing amount of public discussion of politico-economic problems ever since the death of Stalin.

The oldest argument, which was heard occasionally even in the days of Stalin, is about the size of the military budget and the share to be given to each service. Soviet military leaders are not very different from those of other countries. They are never sure that they have enough; they dislike admitting that introduction of new weapons systems can justify cuts in conventional forces. Allied with the proponents of heavy industry, they have resisted proposals to decrease the percentage of G.N.P. devoted to defense and they have been outraged by reductions in military man-power. Consumer-oriented groups naturally advocate a different allocation of resources and have found some support in the top leadership. Malenkov, Khrushchev and Brezhnev have all found it necessary to discuss this controversy in public statements. Any literate inhabitant of the U.S.S.R. must know that the controversy exists and that it has caused divisions in the party and some wavering in the party line. This is not calculated to preserve the image of a monolithic, all-wise leadership.

Even more interesting is the discussion of reform of the Soviet economic system. Every leader since Stalin has recognized that the economy was not performing as well as it should, but none of them has been very certain about the proper remedies. Khrushchev's fluctuating and often contradictory economic policies were probably one of the chief reasons for his ouster. Uncertainty at the top and confusion at the operating level have encouraged Soviet economists to express their views. Since they agree no better than their American counterparts on the best policies to promote healthy economic growth, the result has been a long and increasingly public discussion of such topics as the role of centralized planning, the degree to which market demand should influence production and the effectiveness of present types of collective farming. To discuss these topics is to question some of the basic theories and institutions of Soviet society.

The party has not only tolerated this discussion; at times it actually seems to have welcomed it. It is always possible, of course, that leaders who prefer traditional policies are hoping to give the proponents of innovation enough rope to hang themselves. If so, it is a risky game. This may be one case in which the lie will find it hard to catch up with the truth, and in any event the lack of unanimity among the leadership will have been made painfully evident.

It seems somewhat more likely that the top leadership sees no other way of finding answers to its difficult economic problems. It cannot impose a solution because it doesn't have one. It cannot assemble all the leading Soviet economists in a room and expect them to come up with a unanimous report. Only through a certain amount of public discussion can it get the ideas it needs to reach a decision. Only by experimenting with some of the new proposals can it discover which solutions are desirable. Every new idea and every experiment encourages the formation of groups defending or attacking the innovations. And if economic policy, so fundamental to a Communist state, can be the subject of open discussion and political manoeuvering, what is left that is sacred and untouchable?

When stronger leadership emerges and postponed decisions are made, there will doubtless be an attempt to suppress the present extraordinarily free discussion of economic problems. But the history of the last two decades shows that real differences of opinion are not killed by driving them underground. Powerful interest groups have shown remarkable stubbornness in clinging to their opinions and in surfacing them again as soon as they felt it safe to do so. No one, for example, has ever succeeded in silencing for long the proponents of emphasis on heavy industry, the "steel-eaters," to use Khrushchev's angry phrase. No one has ever kept the military from fighting for bigger, stronger and more expensive forces or from resisting cuts in conventional forces as advanced weapons become more numerous and more effective. A much weaker interest group, the scientists, showed the same stubbornness in the Lysenko case. They would not accept half-measures or a quiet reversal of policy; they kept up their pressure until they had gained an almost complete victory. The debate on economic policy, which has already been mentioned, did not spring full-grown from the cracks in Khrushchev's brain. It was preceded by a long period in which the economists, while outwardly conforming, were becoming more and more convinced that reform, both in economic techniques and economic policy, was necessary.

In short, the Soviet Government cannot function without using these groups; it cannot make sensible decisions without their advice, and it cannot get that advice without allowing some discussion of basic issues. Just as it cannot falsify statistics without creating gross errors in planning and production, so it cannot distort expert opinion without making gross errors in policy. Just as it is beginning to allow some of the mechanisms of the market place to influence the economy in order to improve production, so it is beginning to allow some ideas to be tested in the intellectual market place in order to improve policy. This permissiveness is strictly limited and the limits are subject to change without notice. The party could decide to suppress all public discussion, though only at the price of stagnation and economic inefficiency. It seems more likely, however, that some debate on important issues will continue, and if it continues, it will have a significant impact on the Soviet political system.

As every absolutist government has always known, freedom of discussion, however limited, has inherent dangers. In the first place, if one set of problems can be openly discussed, or if one group of experts is encouraged to voice its opinions, then there is bound to be pressure from other experts to discuss other problems. Moreover, the number of problems and the number of interest groups increase geometrically with the growth of the political and economic complexity of the state. Finally, if administrators and technical experts can express their ideas publicly, others may feel that their opinions should be given some consideration. So far, the ordinary inhabitant of the U.S.S.R. who holds no key position and who can join only party-controlled organizations has had no way of making his voice heard. This does not mean, however, that he can be entirely disregarded.

For one thing, the intellectuals, as in many earlier dictatorships, can express frustration and discontent in subtle and ambiguous language which is hard to control. They stand halfway between the apparatus of the state and the unorganized masses. They have no independent organization; they are not absolutely essential to the state (while scientists and technicians are), and in a pinch they can be either silenced or made to conform. But they do have a place in the kind of society the Soviet leadership envisages, and to silence them is a real confession of defeat. It deprives the ruling group of a potentially valuable asset and it tarnishes the Soviet image abroad, especially in areas like Western Europe where intellectuals are both influential and inclined to favor leftist causes. So in recent years there has been a rather wobbly party line which has given the intellectuals some freedom of expression and allowed them to voice rather strong criticisms of some aspects of the regime. Warnings and occasional crackdowns have not been very effective. The intellectuals are proving to be almost as stubborn as the scientists; as soon as pressure eases they return to forbidden topics. And they have a following. The enormous popularity of poetry readings shows that the intellectuals are providing an outlet for deep-rooted feelings.

Furthermore, there is a public opinion in the U.S.S.R., nebulous, unorganized and powerless though it be. It is doubtful if the Soviet leaders themselves know quite what this public opinion is or how strong it is. But they know it is there, and ever since Malenkov they have tried at times to play upon it. Khrushchev occasionally sounded like an American politician running for office. The present leadership seems less eager to placate the public than he, but it has not abandoned all efforts to persuade and cajole the masses. It is interesting to note also that every leader who has tried to appeal to public opinion has stressed the themes of nationalism and material self-interest, not Marxist ideology.

Here we come to a more important point, the role of the party in assuring the continuity and authority of the leadership. The effectiveness and the degree of responsibility assigned to the party have varied considerably over the years, but it has never ceased to be an efficient agent of political control. On the other hand, it has never been much more than an agency for political control. Soviet leaders have hoped that it could change the thinking of the mass of the population and create the "Soviet man" who accepts without questioning the decisions and requirements of the leadership. They—and especially Khrushchev—have also hoped that the party could stimulate economic growth. But, quite understandably, politicians have not been very successful either as entrepreneurs or as priests. The party's business is to maintain and use its political power, and this it has done effectively. It has preserved its organization; it has survived its factional disputes without any serious loss of authority; it has continued to control access to all positions of power. These are not small accomplishments; on them are based the continued existence and growing power of the Soviet state. But they are not enough to ward off the difficulties which are emerging. The party can undoubtedly keep criticism and dissent from reaching dangerous levels for at least another generation, but it should play more than a policeman's role if it is to make the most of the human resources of the U.S.S.R. Coping with the problems of an increasingly complex society will require the cheerful cooperation of large numbers of people, and this cooperation can be achieved only if the party develops a credo which inspires real enthusiasm. So far it has failed in this task.

Marxist-Leninist doctrine for some time has had little effect on the attitudes and feelings of the people of the U.S.S.R. There are still some party members—Suslov is the most conspicuous example —who are interested in the problems of Communist theory. Even these men at times seem to be engaging in intellectual exercises rather than in the discussion of deeply felt convictions. Most party members are mere careerists who use Marxist doctrine only as a shield to defend their own actions and as a sword against their rivals. The intellectuals think doctrine is boring; the administrative-managerial types find it irrelevant to their problems. The masses do not understand sterile repetitions of the orthodox creed and are not moved by them. Just as the loss of faith in divine right created a demand for a new set of political beliefs in the West, so loss of faith in the infallibility of the leadership and in the doctrines it proclaims requires a new source of inspiration for the U.S.S.R. This need has not yet been met. . . .

All this is not to say that the U.S.S.R. is on the verge of a great upheaval or that it will necessarily become a democracy of the Western type. It also does not imply any weakening of Soviet military power; in fact, if intelligent discussion could solve some of its current economic problems, the U.S.S.R. might be a more formidable opponent than it now is. In any case, a strong political organization has considerable staying power; it can be both harsh and economically inefficient and still survive the resulting criticism and discontent. It can endure for generations, even when the ideology which originally justified its authority is moribund.

It is also true that ideologies have considerable staying power. Even if an ideology seems to be reduced to a set of empty formulae, the mere use of the formulae will influence the style and at times the behavior of those who invoke them. But to say that a process will be slow and uneven is not to say that it will not occur. There are signs of political change in the U.S.S.R.; there is at least a beginning of open discussion of important problems. We know what the eventual results of such discussion were in the West; we should also remember that it was more than a century before the full effect of criticism and discussion was felt. Historical parallels are always dangerous, but they are not always completely misleading. Only in our century has the U.S.S.R. become a modern state. It is hard to believe that it will not repeat some of the experiences of the countries which became modern states three centuries ago.

MICHEL TATU

Economic Reforms and the Decentralization of Power

Michel Tatu has combined scholarly and journalistic careers for many years. A long-time Moscow correspondent for the French newspaper Le Monde, *he has also contributed articles to journals of Soviet affairs. He recently spent several months at the Research Institute on Communist Affairs, Columbia University, where he prepared a study of Soviet history in the last years of the Khrushchev interregnum.*

AT THE END OF SEPTEMBER 1965, the CPSU Central Committee approved a reform in economic management which had been debated in the Soviet Union for close to three years. No one, not even in Moscow, would pretend that the measures adopted in the reform represent a definitive solution to the problems of the Soviet in-

Excerpted from Michel Tatu, "Soviet Reforms: The Debate Goes On," *Problems of Communism* (January-February, 1966), pp. 28–34. Reprinted by permission of the United States Information Agency.

dustrial establishment: rather, they reflect an effort to do what was possible or desirable under the political circumstances of the moment. The Central Committee decision is thus the product of a compromise; yet, to appreciate the importance of the new reform, it is necessary to place it in proper context and to reexamine the great debate that preceded its adoption.

There had long been general agreement that "something had to be done" in order to remedy the serious administrative difficulties which had afflicted the Soviet economy ever since the 1930's. At the same time, however, whenever the question of serious reform had arisen, two sources of conservative opposition to any effort at reform had immediately become apparent: one obstacle was the economic administrators themselves; the other sprang from the special relationship between the latter and the Communist Party.

The men who run the Soviet economy have traditionally been divided between those who favor centralized management and administrative planning and those who advocate increased responsibility and autonomy at the enterprise level. This formula simplifies the terms of the debate, but it refers only to broad principles. For the economic planners in Moscow, however, the question was not just one of renouncing certain important positions—the reform of 1957 had already changed a great many things in this respect—but of giving up methods bequeathed by a quarter century of Stalinist administration. In any case, any move to replace the relatively simple administrative procedures of a command economy with the infinitely less "dependable" indirect levers of the market system (prices, interest, profits) is bound to be a long drawn-out process.

Some more strictly political aspects of economic management have also hindered change. For example, one of the prerequisites of a more efficient planning system in the USSR is a rationalization of industrial prices—an extremely difficult task not only because of its complexity but also because it inevitably calls into question such well-established priorities as the preferential treatment accorded to heavy metallurgy, machine-building and coal production.

The serious obstacles to the reform became readily apparent during the debate provoked in the fall of 1962 by the theses of Professor Ye. Liberman. Even when the discussion remained restricted to economic circles (as was the case with the debate launched toward the end of October 1962 by *Ekonomicheskaia gazeta*), the arguments of the centralizers—mainly representatives of the large economic agencies of the state as well as certain economists—seemed to prevail. The more liberal tendencies were displayed by a minority of until then relatively unknown economists, a few professors from Moscow and the provinces, and several enterprise managers; and even these—suffering from a complete lack of experience in planning under market conditions and believing that significant progress in that direction could not be expected anyway—were really more concerned with simplifying the existing bureaucratic tutelage rather than liquidating it completely. In this sense, the return to ministerial responsibility in national economic management could hardly be expected to displease anyone.

The attitude of the top planners has been more variegated. Thus, ever since the end of 1964, Premier Kosygin has given the impression of lending an attentive ear to the suggestions of the younger economists, while carefully assuring everyone that he supported centralized planning. He has favored the natural tendency of Gosplan to maintain maximum control over industry, but unlike the planning agency, he has also been critical of the methods of management practiced under the Soviet command system. Centralized but rationalized management, depending more strictly on the laws of the market, seems to have been his objective. Furthermore, having long advocated an expansion of the consumer goods industries, Kosygin has fewer reservations than others about reforming the price system. In his speech of March 19, 1965, he showed himself quite strict vis-à-vis his questioners, very hostile towards all dogmatism, but at the same time uncommitted on the subject of enterprise autonomy. Nevertheless, his clear support (expressed earlier at the December 1964 session of the Supreme Soviet) of a system of direct links between enterprises, even in heavy industry, represented a significant blow to the administrative totalitarianism of the planners of the old school.

The resistance to the reform emanating from the party requires a more complex analysis. In principle, the party functionaries are not directly concerned with the dispute, while in fact they busily propagate the slogan "initiative from below." Also, they can afford to be less "centralist" than the top planners in Moscow since a certain degree of local autonomy enables the regional party apparatus to exercise closer control over the economy; only thus can one explain the support for the sovnarkhozes expressed as late as December 1964 by such regional officials as G. I. Popov, the

Leningrad party secretary, and N. G. Yegorychev, his counterpart in Moscow. They are, however, determined not to allow the *khoziaistvenniki* (economic managers) to take upon themselves the role of leaders. This preoccupation is apparent at all levels of the party apparatus.

The problem, in its essence, is the question of the extent to which the party functionaries should become involved in the practical affairs (*konkretnost*) of Soviet economic life. Theoretically, the problem does not exist: the party does not inject itself into the work of the economic cadres, it merely lends its "assistance"; it does not give orders, only "recommendations"; it does not impose personnel changes, it merely "proposes" them. But if one remembers that precisely the same formulas presumably govern the role of the party in other domains of public life from politics to literature, one soon realizes that in practice these subtle distinctions are of little effect.

An effort has thus been made recently to define more closely the desirable equilibrium. In contrast to Khrushchevian practice, which had pushed the confusion of powers almost to the point of a complete takeover of economic functions by the party, one now encounters denunciations of attempts by party authorities to encroach upon the work of economic organs (*podmena*) or engage in "detailed supervision" (*malochnaia opeka*)—terms with which the Soviet public has been familiar for many years. Along with these exhortations, however, the press continues to reassert the old nostrums of Soviet management policy, which inevitably lead to the very excesses that are being so assiduously denounced. A striking example of this occurred last year. On January 4, 1965, *Pravda* gleefully announced that kolkhozes had been given the authority to determine their own sowing plans, but at the same time it complained that "very important crops had been arbitrarily and without serious motive" reduced in acreage. Unabashedly the party paper continued:

Organs of the party, the soviets and agriculture are called upon to direct this work (agricultural planning). Their immediate task is to help rural workers in examining, *from the point of view of the state,* their activity and elaborating the plan. (Emphasis added.)

On June 29, 1965, *Pravda* returned to the attack. It was necessary, said the paper in an editorial, "to trust the specialists," but such "confidence does not mean that one must allow things to go to ruin." The "new" line was set forth as follows:

Naturally, it is not a question of interfering at every turn in the daily work of the specialist or of replacing him. Such practices have been definitively condemned and will not be taken up again. What is necessary, however, is *concrete help, daily and profound control* of the implementation of decisions. (Emphasis added.)

In other words, the party has not given up its chronic tendency to say, in effect: You are free and on your own as long as you do as we please. Supplemented by the Khrushchevian motto, "Trust but verify" (*dovierat no provierat*), this attitude leaves agricultural producers very little freedom of action, and the same applies in the industrial sector. What, indeed, would happen if industrial managers were subjected to no direct administrative controls and were to be guided only by the economic indicators of the market system? And does the concept of party "assistance," which may be justified under the system of command planning, have any application when only economic criteria govern economic decision-making? Would not the managerial class then be tempted to ignore the leading role of the party not only in economic matters but also in the spheres of ideology and politics? And would not other strata of the population be justified in demanding similar enfranchisement?

Within the party leadership, these same questions were discussed, albeit in somewhat more formal doctrinal terms. In the official view, of course, economic problems are only a part of the vast undertaking the party has assumed for the sake of "building communism," and it would not do therefore to "lose sight of the forest for the trees," or succumb—to cite a particularly revealing *Pravda* article by V. P. Stepanov—"to a narrow-minded practicism disregarding the large horizons of the future." In other words, the economists and the managers are expected to remain in a role strictly subordinate to the party leadership. Even the apparently irreproachable rule—enunciated on March 19, 1965, by Kosygin—that economic plans must be formulated exclusively on the basis of economic realities and in consonance with economic aims is not unobjectionable according to Stepanov's doctrine, since the large task is not just to develop an economy but to build communism. For communism "has not yet been accomplished and it still remains to a considerable degree in *the realm of theory rather than reality*."

One must therefore be concerned not only with the question of how to produce more and better, but also *"by what means"*: "not by capitalist methods, but by the conscientious, voluntary and heroic labor of the workers." (Emphasis added.)

All this shows that party officials as a group have shown themselves even less concerned with the need to change the methods of economic management than those charged with strictly economic responsibilities. Among the top leaders, the only exception appears to be Podgorny, who in some of his speeches has taken a strong position in favor of far-reaching reforms. Brezhnev has always been much more vague and appears to have dedicated himself mainly to preaching the "strengthening of the party role in all spheres." Suslov, who even more clearly represents the traditional party apparatus, has not uttered a word on the subject of economic reforms, not even in his wide-ranging speech of June 2, 1965, in Sophia, in which he discussed most of the current problems before the Soviet leadership.

This double obstacle—the attachment of many planners to the prevailing administrative methods and the fears within the party over a possible weakening of its prerogatives—explains why it has been so difficult to launch a "liberal" reform of economic management and why it required so much discussion before the compromise of last September could be reached. It is therefore justifiable to conclude that, partial and insufficient as the latest decisions are, they do represent a handsome victory for the reformers. The results achieved are about all that could be hoped for in the existing political circumstances.

As a result of the September Plenum's decisions, the advocates of managerial autonomy at the enterprise level have scored several gains. Certain centrally-planned indicators in the labor field (number of employees, average wages and productivity) are being abandoned, which may, among other things, make it easier in the future to discharge unproductive workers. Another change involves the replacement of global production indicators by indices relating to output actually sold; this measure is of course designed to improve quality. It should be pointed out, however, that enterprise managers have not won control over the disposition of their products, which will continue to be distributed by the administrative network of "sales and supply centers" (*snabsbyty*), now once again functioning under the central ministries in Moscow. Kosygin has thus been unable to realize his preference for "direct ties" (see his speech of December 1964), and it is most probable that the highly bureaucratized *snabsbyt* system will cause serious difficulties in the future.

In another sector, advances have been achieved in the financial management of enterprises: interest will be charged on state investment funds and loans; the tax on profits is being replaced by a capital stock tax; and, above all, the portion of profit left for free disposal by the enterprise is being increased. On the other hand, the reorganization of the price system—a key step toward rationalization of economic management—has been put off until "1967–68."

As far as central administrative planning is concerned, it remains in force mainly for the purpose of determining the "principal nomenclature" of production, planning new productive capacity, and controlling technological innovation—three areas that involve most of the major decision-making in any economic system. In sum, economic reform in the Soviet Union is still far short not only of establishing a market economy, but even of coming close to the Yugoslav and Czechoslovak economic models, which in principle renounce command planning. . . .

As to the apprehensions felt within the party that its role might be diminished as a result of the reforms, these should by now have been attenuated, particularly insofar as the party's position in the enterprises is concerned; moreover, the "narrow-minded practicism" feared by some party officials is not all-pervasive reality. It is true, to be sure, that the liquidation of the sovnarkhozes eliminates a useful instrument of control over the economy by the regional apparatus of the party, but it should be noted that this mechanism in fact ceased to be very effective in 1963, when the economic regions, with a few exceptions, were enlarged to cover several oblasts, which not only deprived the obkoms of parallel economic institutions but in fact submerged them, in the economic sphere, within vast new administrative structures. Moreover, the Stalinist system of economic ministries, which is now being revived, is sufficiently familiar to everyone so as not to cause any alarm. And finally, at the September Plenum the party received new assurances from Kosygin that the new system of economic administration would "further enhance the guiding role of the party in the economy. The responsibility of the republican central committees, of the kraikoms and of the obkoms will increase considerably."

True, it is still hard to see how the party's role can be reinforced at the regional level, but an article published in the October 4, 1965, issue of *Pravda* suggests that this could be achieved by officially delegating to the regional party committees the horizontal coordinating role which the sovnarkhozes once exercised. The fact is that there are no other bodies today that would be capable of combatting "bureaucratic compartmentalism" (*vedomstvennost*).

At the top echelons of party and state power, the situation is a little more delicate because the reconstitution of numerous and in some instances enormous ministries equipped with vast powers comes on the heels of the suppression—actually effected a year earlier—of the party "bureaus" through which the CPSU Central Committee and Secretariat supervised industry over the preceding years. A formidable army of captains of industry, this time enjoying effective command, is thus about to confront a political apparatus that lacks a recognized leader as well, probably, as solid unity. How many in the party are likely to enjoy this prospect? Reacting to the problem, Brezhnev in his speech before the Central Committee Plenum stressed the role of partkoms in the new ministries; he expects these party bodies to "inform the Central Committee of the CPSU periodically on the progress of work" in the new administrations. Yegorychev, in his *Pravda* article mentioned above, made a similar suggestion. But will such a safeguard be sufficient to assure respect for party authority at this level, especially in view of the fact that complaints are already being heard—from Brezhnev himself among others—that the party decisions of March 1965 on aid to agriculture have been ignored by the planning apparatus?

In sum, then, the reform measures announced last September do not entirely resolve the political problems that have dominated the economic debate of the past months, nor do they even begin to eliminate the fundamental deficiencies of Soviet economic management. Rather, the reformers have had to satisfy themselves with a certain streamlining of the existing system by eliminating superfluous administrative echelons and establishing a clearer division of functions. But the drawbacks of the system remain—even those which drove Khrushchev in 1957 to introduce *his* reform—and they may soon assume an aggravated form, since the Soviet economy has now reached a new and higher level of development and complexity. Under these circumstances, "bureaucratic compartmentalism" is bound to have even more serious effects than before, particularly on the introduction of new technology. Furthermore, it is difficult to see how the new Gosplan will be able to avoid the errors, paralysis, and competing influences of various pressure groups which were so vigorously deplored in the past.

It remains to be seen whether the enterprise managers will learn to utilize those limited rights that they have been granted; many have noticed and criticized the fact (see Kosygin's speech of December 1964) that certain past measures liberalizing management procedures in both agriculture and industry have never been put into effect. This state of affairs can be traced to the equivocal role of the party, to its "guidance" and the resulting politization of economic administration, and also to the attitude of the managers themselves, who under the present system equate prudence with the line of least resistance. To break this inertia, to make people truly believe in the possibility of change and the need for individual initiative, much more radical measures are required. What is needed is an "administrative destalinization" in fact and in spirit. Perhaps the next reform will bring such a breakthrough.

III

Coercion, Persuasion, and the Rule of Law

HAROLD J. BERMAN
The Law and the Soviet Citizen

Harold J. Berman is Professor of Law at Harvard Law School, and an expert on the Soviet legal system. He spent the 1961–62 academic year in the Soviet Union studying at the Institute of State and Law of the Academy of Sciences and lecturing on American law at Moscow State University. His major work in this field is Justice in the USSR: An Interpretation of Soviet Law *(1963). The following selection is a revision of his Arthur T. Vanderbilt Memorial Lecture delivered to the Harvard Law School Association of New Jersey on November 20, 1962.*

I. The Significance of Soviet Law Reform

THE FACT THAT the Soviet concept of social order is not a static but a developing one is dramatically illustrated in the striking changes which have taken place in the Soviet legal system in recent years. Indeed the reform movement in Soviet law is one of the most significant aspects of Soviet social development in the past ten years since Stalin's death.

In interpreting this reform movement, one must start with Stalin —however much the present Soviet leaders would like to expunge his name from the memory of their people. For despite the very substantial changes which they have introduced, the Soviet legal system remains Stalinist in its basic structure and its basic purposes. The organization and functions of the law-making, law-enforcing, and law-practicing agencies—the legislature, the Procuracy, the courts, the administrative organs, the bar—are not essentially different now from what they were when Stalin died. The

From Harold J. Berman, "The Dilemma of Soviet Law Reform," *Harvard Law Review* (March, 1963), pp. 929–951. © 1963 *Harvard Law Review*. Reprinted by permission of the author and publisher.

main outlines of Soviet criminal law and procedure, civil law and procedure, labor law, agrarian law, family law, administrative law, constitutional law, and other branches of the Soviet legal tree, remain basically the same as before.

And if one looks behind the structure to the purposes of Soviet law, it remains a totalitarian law, in the sense that it seeks to regulate all aspects of economic and social life, including the circulation of thought, while leaving the critical questions of political power to be decided by informal, secret procedures beyond the scrutiny or control either of legislative or judicial bodies. It remains the law of a one-party state. It remains the law of a planned economy. It remains a law whose primary function is to discipline, guide, train, and educate Soviet citizens to be dedicated members of a collectivized and mobilized social order.

If this is so, it may be asked, what is the significance of the recent reforms? Indeed, many Western observers have treated each successive development in Soviet law during the past ten years as mere smoke without fire—or even as a smokescreen designed to conceal the absence of any fire. Others have viewed the reforms as half-hearted concessions designed to appease the appetite of the Soviet people without really satisfying their hunger. These grudging responses are reminiscent of Soviet interpretations of American law reforms: the New Deal, we are told by Soviet writers, did not really alter the fundamental nature of the American capitalist system; the Supreme Court decision in the *Segregation Cases* did not end discrimination against Negroes; American law remains "bourgeois."

Viewed from a sufficiently lofty height, the scene never changes. This may only mean, however, that the viewer does not see what is really going on. To give an example: in December 1958 the Supreme Soviet enacted new Fundamental Principles of Criminal Law which, among other things, reduced the maximum period of detention of criminals from twenty-five to fifteen years. This was part of a general movement toward greater leniency in penal policy. In 1961 and 1962, however, the death penalty (which previously had been restricted to certain crimes against the State and to first-degree murder) was extended to various economic crimes, such as bribery of state officials under aggravating circumstances, counterfeiting, illegal transactions in foreign currency, and large-scale theft of state or social property. One of the main reasons for the excessive harshness of 1961–1962 was the disappointment of the Soviet leaders in the results of the excessive softness of 1958, for in fact the rate of serious crimes increased in 1959, 1960, and 1961. The point is that those Western observers who did not take seriously the earlier policy of leniency are in a poor position to evaluate the later policy of repression.

Of course, if the observer abandons all elevation and descends into the midst of the events, he loses all perspective and sees only flux. The foreign journalist in Moscow—and the reader of his articles at home—tend to see a whirling, eddying stream. The only solution is to seek a composite picture, from various perspectives.

Such a composite picture would reveal, I believe, six major tendencies in Soviet law reform since 1953:

First, there has been a tendency toward the elimination of political terror.

Second, there has been a tendency toward the liberalization both of procedures and of substantive norms.

Third, there has been a tendency toward the systematization and rationalization of the legal system.

Fourth, there has been a tendency toward decentralization and democratization of decision-making.

Fifth, there has been a tendency to introduce popular participation in the administration of justice.

Sixth, there has been a tendency in the past two years to threaten those who will not cooperate in building communism with harsh criminal and administrative penalties.

A. THE TENDENCY TOWARD ELIMINATION OF TERROR

Stalin's system since the mid-1930's was based on a coexistence of law and terror. Law was for those areas of Soviet life where the political factor was stabilized. Terror, either naked or in the guise of law (as in the purge trials of the late 1930's), was applied when the regime felt itself threatened. But these two spheres were not easy to keep separate either in theory or in practice. It was not a peaceful coexistence. In the first place, the borderline shifted: the crime of theft of state property, for example, which was supposed to be dealt with by due process of law, could easily merge with counterrevolutionary crime and thereby become subject to repression by the secret police. In the second place, even though terror diminished after 1938, it continued to have a deleterious effect on the legal system itself. Urgently needed law reforms were delayed and sidetracked because of people's fear of being labeled "deviationist."

A month after Stalin's death in March 1953, his successors began to proclaim the "inviolability" of Soviet law and to denounce "arbitrary procedures" and "violations of socialist legality," particularly in connection with the so-called "Doctors' Plot," which many have supposed Stalin trumped up in the last months of his life as a pretext for a new wave of purges. After the arrest of Beria in July 1953, many of the excesses of Stalinist terror were attributed not to the dictator himself but to his chief of secret police. This deception wore thin, however, and in February 1956 Khrushchev attacked Stalin by name at the 20th Congress of the Communist Party of the Soviet Union, denouncing him for the "cult of personality" and for persecution of loyal party members in violation of their legal rights. In October-November 1961, at the 22nd Party Congress, the attacks on Stalin were renewed with even greater vigor. The inviolability of socialist law was again proclaimed. Vyshinsky's name was added to Stalin's as co-author of a legal system which permitted falsification and distortion of legality for the persecution of people innocent of any crime.

In implementation of these attacks upon the "cult of personality," important steps have been taken since September 1953 to eliminate those features of the preexisting Soviet law which permitted the disguise of terror in legal form.

First, the Special Board of the Ministry of Internal Affairs has been abolished. It was this Special Board which had been the chief instrument of terror. It was a three-man administrative committee—the Russians called it a *troika*—which was empowered by a 1934 statute to send people to labor camps without a hearing, in a secret administrative procedure, without right of counsel and without right of appeal.

Second, the security police have been deprived of the power to conduct investigations of crimes under their own special rules without supervision by the Procuracy.

Third, the special procedures for court cases involving the most serious antistate crimes have been abolished. The laws of 1934 and 1937 permitting persons charged with certain such crimes to be tried secretly, in absentia, and without counsel, were repealed.

Fourth, the military courts, which had previously had a wide jurisdiction over civilians, particularly in the case of political crimes, have been deprived of all jurisdiction over civilians except for espionage.

Fifth, the law permitting punishment of relatives of one who deserts to a foreign country from the armed forces—though they knew nothing of the desertion—has been abolished.

Sixth, Vyshinsky's doctrine that confessions have special evidentiary force in cases of counterrevolutionary crimes—based on the transparently false notion that people will not confess to such crimes unless they are actually guilty—has been repudiated; confessions are now treated as having no evidentiary force in themselves, and the matters contained in a confession must be corroborated by other evidence.

Seventh, Vyshinsky's doctrine that the burden of proof shifts to the accused in cases of counterrevolutionary crimes has also been repudiated. The new Soviet codes place the burden of proving the guilt of the accused squarely on the prosecutor. Although the phrase "presumption of innocence" is avoided in the codes, all that we mean by that phrase is spelled out in Soviet law.

Eighth, Vyshinsky's broad definition of complicity, borrowed from the Anglo-American doctrine of conspiracy, has been repudiated. Innocent association with others who are planning an illegal act can no longer constitute a crime under the new Soviet legislation.

Ninth, the law on so-called "counterrevolutionary crimes" has been slightly narrowed and made a little less vague. The term "counterrevolutionary" has been eliminated and the term "anti-state" substituted. The crime of "terrorist acts," which hitherto had been interpreted to include any violent act against a state or party official or, indeed, his close relatives, whatever the motive, has been restricted to murder or serious bodily injury of the official himself committed for the purpose of overthrowing or weakening the Soviet authority. The law on state secrets has been substantially relaxed—though it is still far wider in its scope than we would consider tolerable. And a new list of information constituting state secrets has been enacted which is less broad and more precise than the earlier list.

Finally, there took place from 1953 (or 1955) to 1957 a systematic reexamination of all cases of persons previously convicted of counterrevolutionary crimes and the release from labor camps of the overwhelming majority of such persons as fully rehabilitated.

The restoration of procedural due process of law in political cases is a signal achievement of the post-Stalin regime. The Soviet citizen is now protected against police terror, false charges, and faked trials to a far greater extent than ever before in Soviet history. No longer need he fear the midnight knock on the door as a prelude to transportation to a Siberian labor camp without a fair hearing.

Yet one cannot speak of the total elimination of political terror so long as open opposition to Communist Party policy—the "Party line"—can lead to criminal sanctions, however "objectively" and "correctly" imposed. The 1958 Statute on State Crimes carries over from the earlier law on counterrevolutionary crimes the provision against "agitation or propaganda" directed against the Soviet system. To defame the Soviet political and social system, or even to possess written materials of such defamatory nature, if for the purpose of weakening Soviet authority, is punishable by deprivation of freedom of up to seven years. In 1961, for example, certain leaders of the Jewish community in Leningrad were convicted for the crime of circulating anti-Soviet literature obtained from a foreign embassy, presumably the Israeli. We would call this a denial of "substantive" due process of law.

The law of antistate agitation and propaganda is only one of many features of the Soviet system which keep alive the fear of Soviet citizens that the terror may return. Later I shall speak more fully of this fear, and of some of the conditions which give rise to it. But it is important to stress at this point that the fear of a return to terror is itself a form of terror. Therefore, one must view the developments of the past ten years as reflecting only a tendency—though an extremely important tendency—toward the elimination of terror.

B. THE LIBERALIZATION OF PROCEDURAL AND SUBSTANTIVE LAW

Even apart from political crimes, Soviet law has undergone substantial liberalization in the past ten years. It would be impossible to list the hundreds, indeed thousands, of needed reforms which have been introduced. Let me speak very briefly of some of the most important, first in criminal law and procedure, then in criminal punishment and the system of detention, and finally in some other fields of law.

In criminal law and procedure, the "tightening up" of the rules with respect to burden of proof, evaluation of confessions, and the doctrine of complicity, which have already been mentioned in the discussion of political crimes, have given increased protection to persons accused of other crimes as well. In addition, the right to counsel prior to trial, though still limited, has been significantly extended, the time for supervisory review of acquittals in criminal cases, formerly unlimited, has been reduced to one year; powers of search and seizure have been somewhat restricted; the doctrine of analogy, whereby a person who committed a socially dangerous act not specifically made punishable by law could be sentenced under a law proscribing an analogous act, has been eliminated; penalties have been substantially lightened for many crimes—for example, new laws imposing lighter sentences for petty rowdyism ("hooliganism") and petty theft of state or public property have removed the necessity of many long years in labor camps for conviction of trivial offenses; and some crimes have been eliminated altogether—for example, abortion, absenteeism from work, and quitting one's job without permission. The large-scale amnesties of 1953 and 1957 released all except those sentenced for, or charged with, the most serious offenses.

With respect to the system of detention, a 1957 law eliminated the name "labor camp," substituting "labor colony" for all places of confinement (except prisons, which are used only for temporary detention or, very rarely, for the most serious crimes) and introduced a new regime for prisoners which permits far more leniency in their treatment. Those convicted of less serious crimes are permitted to have their wives (or husbands) visit and stay with them from time to time; they are paid substantial wages for their work and are required to send home allotments to their dependents. Also liberal parole provisions have been introduced.

Liberalization has not been confined to criminal policy. Since 1953, and especially since 1955, there has been a reexamination of every branch of law and a weeding out of many of the harshest features. For example, a new civil right has been created to obtain a court order for public retraction of a newspaper libel. Equal rights of foreigners under Soviet law have been declared—subject, of course, to statutory restrictions. (It would be interesting to put those two provisions together and to have a suit by a foreigner in a Soviet court demanding a retraction of a newspaper libel against him.) In labor law the rights of trade unions have been enhanced and the procedures for settlement of workers' grievances have been improved. In family law, a new code is expected to be enacted shortly which will, among other things, ameliorate the position of the child born out of wedlock. Similar examples could be multiplied from many other fields of law.

In 1961 and 1962 there has been a contrary trend, away from liberalization, in certain areas. These recent backward steps, however, cannot, yet at least, be considered to have stopped the liberal momentum of the post-Stalin reforms.

C. SYSTEMATIZATION AND RATIONALIZATION

The general tendency toward liberalization of law is, of course, an important supporting buttress of the tendency toward elimination of political terror. For such tendencies to have permanence, however, deeper foundations are required in the legal system as a whole. From that standpoint, the efforts of recent years to systematize and rationalize the Soviet legal system are of great significance.

The Stalin Constitution of December 1936, and the Vyshinsky jurisprudence which surrounded it, rehabilitated the various republican criminal, civil, labor, and family codes of the "New Economic Policy" period of the twenties which had largely fallen into disrepute in the period from 1930 to 1936. Of course the NEP codes, designed for a transition period of mixed capitalism-socialism, were inadequate for the new period of full socialism with its planned economy. The Stalin Constitution therefore called for the creation of all-union codes to replace the earlier republican codes. But until such new all-union codes were adopted, the earlier ones were to prevail, together with the thousands of statutory and administrative changes introduced into them.

During the remaining sixteen years of Stalin's reign, however, new all-union codes were not adopted, although many drafts were produced. Only with the removal of the political and ideological pressure of Stalinist autocracy did it become possible to introduce new codes, and, together with them, a reorganization of the entire system of legal administration.

The first major event in this development was the adoption in August 1955 of a new Statute on Procuracy Supervision. The procuracy is the cornerstone of the Soviet legal system. It combines functions of our Department of Justice, congressional investigating committees, and grand juries. It not only investigates and prosecutes crimes, but it supervises the entire system of administration of justice, and has power to investigate and protest to higher authorities (whether administrative or judicial) any abuse of law which comes to its attention. Until 1955 it had operated on the basis of a 1922 statute upon which were encrusted many legislative and administrative modifications. The 1955 statute clarified and consolidated its supervisory powers over judicial and administrative acts. Incidentally, the new statute also added sanctions against officials of the Procuracy for negligence in failing to expose illegal practices in places of detention of criminals.

The second major event was the removal of certain aspects of Ministry of Justice control over the courts, and the reorganization of the Supreme Court of the U.S.S.R. and of the republican and regional courts. This took place in 1956 and 1957. The result was a streamlining of the court system and an increase in its independence.

In 1957 the constitution was amended to provide for separate republican codes to be based upon new all-union Fundamental Principles. In December 1958 the Supreme Soviet of the U.S.S.R. adopted a series of Fundamental Principles of various branches of law—Fundamental Principles of Criminal Law, Fundamental Principles of Criminal Procedure, and Fundamental Principles of Court Organization—together with new comprehensive statutes on state crimes, military crimes, and military tribunals. Subsequently, in December 1961, the Supreme Soviet adopted Fundamental Principles of Civil Law and of Civil Procedure. Fundamental Principles of Family Law and of Labor Law are now in preparation; indeed, a statute on the procedure for the hearing of labor disputes adopted in 1957 is itself a systematization of many aspects of labor law.

On the basis of the Fundamental Principles, the various republics have adopted their own new codes of criminal law and criminal procedure and are now in the last stages of work on new codes of civil law and civil procedure. . . .

The systematization and rationalization of Soviet law is not something which can be accomplished in a few years. Indeed, it is something which must go on continually. The recognition of its importance, and the very great efforts being devoted to it, are an encouraging sign of the determination of the post-Stalin regime to establish a far higher degree of legal security than that which existed in the past.

D. THE TENDENCY TOWARD DECENTRALIZATION AND DEMOCRATIZATION

Khrushchev has committed himself to the view that the harshness of the Stalinist system cannot achieve the purposes of socialism as he envisages it, and that cooperation with the policies of his regime cannot be secured without a systematic and rational legality. Implicit in this conviction, and necessary to its implementation, is the belief in the possibility of a wide decentralization of decision-making and a still wider participation of the public in the formulation of issues for decision.

Two qualifications must be made at the outset, however, in discussing the tendency of the post-Stalin period of Soviet history toward greater decentralization and democratization. The first is that there is no sign that the present Soviet leadership has any intention of allowing this tendency to go beyond its power to control it. The limits of decentralized decision-making and democratization are set by the central authorities. The second qualification is that this theory of "democratic centralism"—centralization of authority combined with decentralization of operations—was also Stalin's theory. The difference today is a difference in degree.

The tendency toward decentralization and democratization has been greatly accelerated since Stalin's death, however, by the very nature of the tendencies toward elimination of political terror, toward liberalization, and toward systematization and rationalization of the law. Apart from all other considerations, these tendencies have imposed an absolute requirement of help from hundreds of thousands of people at various levels of the official hierarchy and in various parts of the Soviet Union. In addition, the main purpose of these tendencies—to overcome the rigidities of the system inherited from Stalin, to stimulate local and individual initiative and enthusiasm—has necessitated the enlistment of maximum cooperation from the maximum number of people. . . .

The decision in 1957 to abandon the rule of the 1936 Constitution calling for all-union codes and to substitute a rule calling for separate codes in each of the fifteen Soviet republics, based, however, on all-union Fundamental Principles; the earlier decision to dissolve the all-union Ministry of Justice into separate republican ministries of justice and the later decision to do the same with the Ministry of Internal Affairs; and, most important of all, the decision in 1957 to split the economy of the country into about one hundred economic regions, each with its own Council of National Economy, and to divide among these regional councils some of the functions of the former economic ministries with their central offices in Moscow—these decisions in the direction of decentralization were called for by the enormous bureaucratization of Soviet social and economic life, which had become almost too stifling to endure.

Yet decentralization in itself is not democratization; it may be, and to a certain extent it has been, simply a moving of the center to the localities, a stretching of the chain of command. It has also been more than that, however. The lower links in the chain have unquestionably been given more initiative. And even where ultimate decisions have been reserved for Moscow, a far greater hearing has been given to the voices of the localities.

This is illustrated by the process of law reform itself, Khrushchev and his immediate associates could give the word that the time had come for substantial law reforms and could indicate the lines along which the reforms should run. But the word could not become a reality without an enormous effort by the people who would be directly affected by these reforms. These include not only the professional lawyers who would have to draft them and the officials who would have to administer them, but also the various people who would have to live under them.

The comprehensive legislation enacted in recent years has been worked on by representatives of hundreds, indeed thousands, of organizations. All the major governmental agencies have expressed detailed views on their various provisions. There has been endless discussion of them in the universities, in research institutes, in economic organizations of various kinds, in scholarly journals, and in the daily press. . . .

In addition, popular participation in lawmaking has been stimulated by the expansion of the committee system of the Supreme Soviet of the U.S.S.R. and of the Supreme Soviets of the fifteen republics. Tens of thousands of expert consultants have reported to these committees. And apart from major all-union and republican legislation, there has been a substantial increase in the powers of the local municipal councils and a vast amount of activity of local governmental organizations, involving the participation of literally hundreds of thousands of Soviet citizens.

Of course it would be a mistake to suppose that Soviet federalism and Soviet democracy involve—as ours do—a struggle between opposing political units and groups, a competition for political leadership. In the Soviet Union all power resides in the Communist Party, which remains, as stated in the constitution, the "central core" of all organizations, whether they be state organizations or social organizations. Despite the development of greater intra-Party democracy in recent years, the Party remains a disciplined elite, subservient to its leadership. Decentralization and democratization of decision-making in the spheres of government, law, and economic administration is not a threat to Party supremacy; indeed it is required by the Party as a means of maintaining its supremacy.

Yet Party control is, in a much deeper sense, challenged by the development of autonomous centers of discussion and initiative, even though it remains the "central core" of such centers. One of my strongest impressions in a year of intimate association with Soviet jurists of all kinds is that of their cohesion. Whether they are judges, procurators, Ministry of Justice officials, law professors, research workers, legal advisers of state institutions and enterprises, or advocates, the seventy to eighty thousand jurists of the Soviet Union are bound together by the closest professional ties. They meet together in many different kinds of activity; they discuss and debate common problems; they work together; and they are bound not only by their common legal education but also by their common vested interest in the preservation of legality. As a class, they have grown greatly in importance during the past ten years.

E. POPULAR PARTICIPATION IN THE ADMINISTRATION OF JUSTICE

. . . It is Soviet theory that under communism the functions of state organizations (which operate in part by coercion) will be turned over entirely to social organizations (which operate only by persuasion). In anticipation of this glorious day, the role of social organizations has been greatly increased. Neighborhood and factory meetings have been convened for a variety of purposes and have been given certain semijudicial functions. Also a voluntary auxiliary police force has been organized—the so-called *druzhiny,* or bands—to help keep order; they direct traffic, take drunks into custody, and in general make themselves unpopular among the people on the streets. In addition, many special volunteer commissions have been formed and given semi-official status—to observe conditions in the labor colonies and to make recommendations, to report to municipal councils on housing questions, to report on local observance of "socialist legality," and for a host of similar purposes. Trade unions and the Young Communist League (*Komsomol*) are also considered to be social organizations, and their functions have been extended.

Many of the functions of Soviet social organizations are also performed in the United States by volunteer workers and social organizations. Indeed, no country in the world can match the United States, I would venture to say, in the amount of public-spirited activity of volunteer social organizations. Yet there is a difference in kind between Soviet social organizations and their American counterparts—a difference which is striking. In part it is a difference in the scope of the activities of Soviet social organizations and especially their powers over the lives of their members; in part it is a difference in the amount of official pressure that can be brought upon them, due especially to their links with the State through the Communist Party. . . .

[An] example may be found in the activities of "comrades' courts," now operating under a recent statute, which meet in apartment houses or in factories to consider minor offenses committed by neighbors or fellow-workers. Their punitive powers are limited to a ten-ruble fine. Mostly they issue reprimands and warnings. However, they may also recommend eviction from the apartment or disciplinary action (including demotion) by the factory management. Such eviction or disciplinary action may be resisted through regular court proceedings, but nevertheless the recommendation of the comrades' court is a serious matter. One other example: Soviet courts sometimes go "on circuit," so to speak, to apartments or factories, to hear criminal cases involving persons in those places. The purpose is to demonstrate to the entire "collective" and to the public the social danger of the offenses charged and to educate people in the requirements of the law. But the tendency to convict and to mete out harsh punishment is very strong when such an educational purpose is in the forefront of the procedure itself.

Some Western students of the Soviet scene have, in my opinion, exaggerated the evils of this kind of new "social justice." One must put oneself in the Soviet situation, where true social cooperation in informal voluntary groups, entirely independent of the State, hardly exists. The comrades' courts that I have seen in action have impressed me by the good spirit with which they act and with which they are received. Especially important is the fact that their powers are very limited and that these limits are enforced by the courts and by the legal system.

The great danger, of course, is the potentiality of abuse of these social organizations by the Communist Party and the State. The still greater danger is the dream of a far-off time when there will be no legal system and no State but only one vast social organization, one vast Communist Party. It is, I am sure, a dream which can never be realized; but so long as it is held it inhibits the achievement of true legal security.

F. THE RETURN TO HARSH CRIMINAL
AND ADMINISTRATIVE PENALTIES

A sixth major tendency in Soviet law in the post-Stalin period is the return in 1961 and 1962 to harsh criminal and administrative penalties against those who refuse to cooperate in building communism.

In May and June 1961, the three largest republics, comprising three-fourths of the Soviet population, finally enacted the notorious antiparasite law which had been first proposed for public discussion in 1957 and later adopted in the smaller republics from 1957 through 1960. This law, in its final form, provides for "resettlement" in specially designated localities, for two to five years, of persons who constitute "antisocial, parasitic elements" and who are not performing socially useful work but are living on unearned income. Persons may be sentenced under this law by the judges of the regular courts in a summary procedure and without the usual guarantees of the criminal law, or else by general meetings in the factories or apartments, with review by the local municipal council.

In 1959 I was told in Moscow by the principal draftsman of the 1958 Fundamental Principles of Criminal Procedure that in his opinion the antiparasite laws contradicted the provision of the Fundamental Principles that no person may be punished for a crime except by sentence of a court; and that there was a good chance they would not be adopted in the three largest republics and that they would be repealed in those republics where they had already been adopted. His optimism proved unjustified. The laws have now been reconciled with the Fundamental Principles on the more-than-tenuous theory that the offender is not being punished for a crime, nor is he being confined; he is simply sent to another place where he must take a socially useful job!

In the first year of the operation of this law in the R.S.F.S.R., as I learned last May at a lecture by the Minister of Justice, 10,000 people in Moscow were charged under the antiparasite law. Eight thousand, he said, received only warnings; 2,000 were sent out of Moscow; of these, only fifteen were subjected to confiscation of property. It may be inferred from the relatively few instances of confiscation that the law is principally a device for getting rid of vagrants and putting them to work.

Also the extension of the death penalty in 1961 and 1962 to a wide variety of crimes, many of them economic crimes not involving violence, reflects the regime's determination to take extreme measures against those who most flagrantly violate the tenets of Communist morality. In a case tried in July 1961, one of the statutes imposing the death penalty was applied retroactively by a special edict of the Presidium of the Supreme Soviet authorizing the retroactive application "as an exception" in the specific case. (The edict was never published as it was not considered to be "of general significance." I was shown it, however, by a member of the U.S.S.R. Supreme Court. There is reason to believe that there were other such cases of retroactive application of the death sentence, specially authorized by similar edicts.) Judging from Soviet press accounts of individual trials probably over 250 Soviet citizens were executed for economic and other crimes in the year from May 1961 to May 1962, and probably an equal or greater number were executed from June to December 1962. One can only say "probably" because Soviet crime statistics are a state secret! (In 1961, forty-three persons were executed in the United States.)

This harsh policy was also reflected in increased penalties for lesser crimes. Soviet jurists have publicly criticized the tendency of some procurators and courts to treat the imposition of the death penalty for serious crimes as a signal for reversing the entire trend toward liberalization.

What significance should we attach to these developments? As is so often the case with violations of basic principles of judicial procedure, the particular individual victims do not command our affection. They were, presumably, scoundrels. It is rather the abuse of the integrity of the legal process that concerns us, for one abuse suggests another.

When I asked how he could explain the decision of July 1961 applying the death penalty retroactively, one leading Soviet jurist replied, "We lawyers didn't like it!"—an answer as interesting for the "we lawyers" as the "didn't like it." Another prominent lawyer told me he did not believe in the use of the death penalty in peacetime in any case. Not only lawyers, however, were concerned about these measures. An engineer said to me when I raised the question of what was so bad about getting rid of the scoundrels: "If they start with scoundrels, what is to stop them from going on to political opponents?" Whether the majority of Soviet citizens make this connection, however, is something that cannot be known. Many, at least, seem to support the regime's new policy of ruthless repression of large-scale economic crimes.

II. Conclusion

We have heard much of "the thaw"—to use Ehrenberg's phrase —the unfreezing of Soviet life in the years since Stalin died, the reduction of terror, the increased freedom to criticize, the greater encouragement of individual initiative, the relaxation of tensions. But the *long-range* problem of government in the Soviet Union is whether the Soviet leaders are willing and able to establish not merely a season, or a climate, or a policy, of freedom and initiative, but also a legal and institutional foundation which will make freedom and initiative secure from their own intervention. Until that problem is solved, the fear of a return to Stalinist terror will haunt the Soviet people, and especially the intellectuals. In research institutes and universities, as well as among educated people generally, debates rage over the "liquidation of the consequences of the cult of personality," which is Party jargon for preventing a recurrence not only of violence but also of all the rigidities that went with it. Nobody—presumably from Khrushchev on down—wants such a recurrence. But nobody can guarantee that it won't happen—if it becomes "necessary."

LEONARD SCHAPIRO

Prospects for the Rule of Law

Leonard Schapiro is on the faculty of the London School of Economics and Political Science, London University. Formerly a practicing attorney and still a member of the London Bar Association, he turned to full-time teaching and research in 1955, participating extensively in London University's Russian studies program. He is the author of several books, including The Origin of the Communist Autocracy (1956) *and* The Communist Party of the Soviet Union (1960), *and is also editor of* The USSR and the Future (1962).

Excerpted from Leonard Schapiro, "Prospects for the Rule of Law," *Problems of Communism* (March–April, 1965), pp. 2–7. Reprinted by permission of the United States Information Agency.

THE DEATH OF STALIN set in motion a great wave of enthusiasm—in words, if not in deeds—for the reform of Soviet law. In fact, the fashion for "liberalism" in law reform considerably antedated the official denunciation of Stalin in 1956. But concrete results were rather slower to materialize than some of the promises had suggested. Even so, the special powers of the MVD were abolished in 1953; the powers of the procurators were extended and redefined in 1955; and in 1958 the long-awaited new codes of criminal law and procedure were initiated with the enactment by the Supreme Soviet of the "Fundamental Principles" on which they were to be modelled. These "Fundamental Principles," though far from perfect, were a very considerable improvement on anything hitherto enacted in the Soviet Union on criminal law and procedure and, if implemented, could have provided the basis for some kind of civilized legal practice. . . .

It is perhaps difficult for dictators to get accustomed to the idea that the main purpose of the law is, in fact, to make their task more difficult. The CPSU, in particular, has a long tradition of treating law as something to be disregarded whenever necessary—which is the practical manifestation of the party's theoretical position on the subordination of law to party policy. . . . Khrushchev and his associates seem to have had a genuine enough intention to clean up the Augean stables of Stalinism in the realm of law as well as in other fields. They were, however, faced with a number of strong pressures tempting them to disregard the law and to resort to the old-fashioned practices which we usually associate with the government of the USSR: a tradition of lawlessness; a growing crime rate which the USSR shares with other postwar industrial countries; a growing wave of "speculation," which is often merely a pejorative term for the attempts of the more enterprising to survive in the face of the inefficiency of an overbureaucratized system; and the pressure of the party *apparatchiki* to be allowed to continue their traditional practices for fear that the whole system would otherwise crash about their ears. Much of the material studied in the accompanying articles is in fact devoted to the retrograde developments which in so many instances have followed upon the promising legislation of Christmas Day, 1958. These developments can be summarized quite briefly.

First of all, the experience of the past six years has shown that once the authorities are determined to do so, there still is nothing to prevent them from flagrantly flouting their own laws. [This was demonstrated in a recent] case in which a law imposing the death penalty for certain economic crimes was retroactively applied to a crime committed before the passage of the law. What is so shocking about this case, in this author's view, is not only that it was in direct violation to the Fundamental Principles of 1958, but that judges, procurators, the bar and the party all cooperated to perpetrate this barbarity without—so far as one knows—a word of protest from anyone.

In the absence of full reporting of court cases in the Soviet Union, it is impossible to say how frequent cases of this nature have been, but it would appear from the publicity occasionally given to one of them, or at any rate tolerated by the party authorities, that there are still many Soviet judges and procurators who treat the law and legal machinery as adjuncts of administrative policy. The weekly economic organ of the Central Committee carried an article some months ago criticizing a case in which a young woman, guilty—according to the express terms of the indictment itself—of nothing more than carelessness, had been sentenced to ten years' imprisonment for theft. The judge who had sentenced her, when approached by the reporter who wrote the article, expressed innocent surprise that the woman was still in jail. He had "naturally" sentenced her for theft, he explained, because there had been a local campaign against embezzlement in progress, "but the Supreme Court ought to have put us right."

Another major retrograde step from the 1958 position has been the extensive development of what Professor Leon Lipson . . . has happily called the "Non-Courts and Impolice"—referring to the semi-administrative tribunals and procedures by means of which the Soviet authorities are attempting to deal with those whose anti-social behavior the system condemns, such as the idlers, the parasites, the work-shy, and so forth. One can recognize the magnitude of the problem facing the authorities in this area without sympathizing with the means they are employing to deal with it. It is obvious to any lawyer that procedures of this kind . . . are open to the gravest abuses. Where there are no strict legal safeguards and procedure is what is euphemistically called "informal," the subjective element and the private vendetta become apparent before long. The account of the Brodsky case, recently published in the *New Leader* thanks to the courage of the Soviet journalist who made it available outside the USSR, is an example of what can go on in these "non-courts." It is only fair to observe that many Soviet lawyers share in the disapproval of these procedures, and they have apparently been able to exercise sufficient pressure to get a majority of anti-parasite cases transferred to the regular People's Courts from the folk-meetings provided for by the statutes as an alternative procedure. (Hopefully, some of the regular court judges have a little more sense of proper judicial behavior, or a little more civic courage, than the lady who tried Brodsky.) The Soviet press has also on occasion singled out for criticism—and, one hopes, for restitution—particularly scandalous cases of abuse of the anti-parasite procedure for motives of private vendetta.

A third retrograde step has been the extension of the death penalty during 1961–62 to a wide range of crimes for which no civilized penal system today applies this penalty. All in all, in the course of eleven months, capital punishment was extended to almost as many offenses, including bribery and illegal currency trans-actions. . . . It is idle to justify this severity in penal policy as con-nected in some way with the "socialist" policy of the Soviet state —unless it is the intention of the authorities to depopulate the country by shooting the "non-socialists," whose offenses are very often dictated simply by their strong desire to escape the meshes of bureaucratic control which the state wishes to impose upon every one of its citizens. The treatment of economic crimes in the Soviet Union has recently been the object of a study by the Inter-national Commission of Jurists. This study concludes that the "concentration of law and propaganda on the suppression of eco-nomic crimes evidenced a serious modern malaise in Soviet so-ciety," and that "private enterprise, honest and dishonest, but in both cases illegal, has been carried on in the very heart of pub-lic enterprises." The report also concludes, in view of the dispro-portionate number of Jews sentenced to death for economic crimes, that antisemitism "is possibly being used by the Soviet authorities as a weapon to render unpopular economic offenses. . . ."

Quite apart from these retrogressions from the promising begin-nings of 1958, there are inherent in the Soviet legal and constitu-tional systems certain built-in defects which particularly lend them-selves to abuses for administrative purposes. There is a delusion among some Western writers that the Soviet legal and constitu-tional systems are "all right" on paper, but are merely not ob-served in practice. The trouble is, however, that they are far from "all right" on paper, and there are many ways in which the new Soviet leaders—if such should be their intention—could institutionally improve the constitution, which is now in process of revision. For one thing, the "human rights" provisions will remain worthless so long as there exists no method by which the Soviet citizen can call upon the courts to enforce them. This requires, first, some form of judicial review, some method by which laws and administrative acts which contravene the constitution can be set aside by the courts; and secondly, some method by which the courts can be invoked to constrain officials who evade the constitution.

It goes without saying that such a development in the USSR remains improbable unless and until the Soviet party and state authorities recognize the need for an independent judiciary—and this means judges who not only are independent of actual party pressure at all levels, but who (unlike some of those referred to above) are sufficiently convinced of their independence to go against what they believe to be the "climate of opinion," even where no actual pressure has been brought to bear on them. There would also have to be some kind of constitutional court—the new Yugoslav Constitution, incidentally, contains a provision for such a court and, by this fact alone, is well in advance of the constitutions of the other "socialist" states. Under the Soviet Constitution as it now stands, . . . the state alone remains the sole source of all rights enjoyed by the individual; and what the state can bestow it can also take away. It is impossible for these rights to be secure unless and until the state is prepared, in the interests of legal order, to create some more solid basis for that security.

The weakness of the constitutional position is not the only obstacle to the development of the rule of law, though it is probably the most important one. I should be inclined to list three more: first and foremost, there is the present inquisitorial system of preliminary investigation of crimes—not peculiar, be it said, only to the Soviet legal system—under which, when once the indictment is framed at the conclusion of an investigation, the court inevitably tends to become little more than a rubber stamp. Secondly, there is the absence of a judicial tradition in the Soviet Union. What of such a tradition had been built up before 1917, in the very restricted area of action permitted to it, was virtually destroyed by Lenin and the Bolsheviks as one of their first actions, and very little of it remains. The ethics of judicial behavior, the presumption of innocence, the rule of natural law against the retrospective application of legislation—all these and like aspects of Western judicial tradition seem to be alien to judges and lawyers in Soviet conditions. These habits come of long practice and cannot be induced either by pious exhortations or by decrees. And finally, there is the low status of the Soviet advocate. . . . Whatever the popular attitude towards the lawyer, in the eyes of the authorities he is still an object of suspicion and contempt rather than respect. Yet without a courageous and independent bar of established social status, no real development of the rule of law is conceivable in any society.

The picture, however, is not all black. The worst that can happen to the rule of law in a totalitarian state is what happened under Stalin: the constant and systematic practice of the most flagrant illegality, accompanied by a carefully-drilled, obedient and sycophantic chorus of public men, including practicing and academic lawyers, boasting that the most perfect legality in the world was to be found in the Soviet Union. This is very far from being the situation today. There is still a good deal of illegality, to be sure, but it is nothing to compare with what went on under Stalin. There is also a good deal of criticism, and this gives rise to some hope of further improvement in the future.

It is true that diatribes against illegality started already in Lenin's day, though it was Lenin himself who created (and, so far as one knows, never disapproved) the position above the law that was assumed by his party. The occasional blasts in the party journals today in favor of "socialist legality" should not therefore be treated too seriously, or be expected to have much effect on practice whenever the party finds that violating the law is a convenient expedient for imposing its policy. But the criticism of the last few years has not been confined to conventional party exhortations. On the contrary, it has been such as to indicate that a strenuous debate is going on under the surface of Soviet society in the field of law as in other fields. The issues ventilated in newspaper articles, especially in *Izvestia,* recur with a regularity which suggests that certain topics are being constantly pressed by advocates of the rule of law whenever the opportunity arises. The criticisms of individual miscarriages of justice have been sharp, derisory, and above all quite unsparing of important individuals, even persons in high party office. Some of the most hallowed traditions of Soviet lawlessness have been attacked. It may be that not all these efforts have been in vain. A hopeful sign, for instance, was a recent article by the Chairman of the Supreme Court of the USSR, which in a number of important respects departs from the familiar official sermon on "socialist legality."

This article contains several points of interest. Much of it is devoted to support of the proposition that the preliminary investigation of a crime should not be treated as the trial, with the subsequent court proceedings merely serving to endorse a foregone conclusion. "None of the conclusions of the preliminary investigation," writes Chairman Gorkin, "are binding on the court," which must carefully and publicly investigate the evidence on its own responsibility. The significance of this is that it endorses a proposition which has been argued for years by an eminent Soviet academic jurist, Professor M. M. Strogovich. Strogovich has advocated a number of basic improvements in Soviet legal practice but has hitherto met invariably with official criticism and even abuse—he has been accused both of subservience to bourgeois law and of subservience in the past to Stalin and Vyshinsky. In his recent article, however, Gorkin singles out Strogovich's view on the subject of preliminary investigation for praise and dismisses the views of those who have attacked him. One can only hope that this marks the beginning of a new attitude on the part of the Soviet establishment towards some of the more conscientious and courageous academic lawyers.

One other point of unusual interest in Gorkin's article deserves mention. This is his attack on the hallowed Soviet practice whereby, the moment someone is accused of a crime, the press assumes his guilt and begins demanding an exemplary penalty. This practice, says Gorkin, can often have the effect of encouraging miscarriages of justice that might otherwise be prevented. Coming as it does from the highest judicial authority in the USSR, Gorkin's article could conceivably have a salutary influence in instilling in Soviet judges a greater sense of civic courage.

Although Strogovich is the only really liberal academic lawyer to have received such an unusual accolade of official approval, there are several others who have been able to make their views heard—and the extent to which such liberal views win official endorsement in the future will be a measure of the extent to which the new Soviet leaders intend to encourage the development of better legal habits. Two professors in particular come to mind—O. S. Ioffe and M. D. Shargorodski. In the course of 1963, these two scholars seem to have aroused official displeasure by the zeal with which they urged the need for regular observance of legal norms in Soviet society. In a joint article published in April 1963, they based their argument on the proposition that, with the replacement of the dictatorship of the proletariat by the state of the whole people, there is no longer any class left to repress; and that the people can achieve the maximum development of their potentialities only on the basis of fixed and regular norms of law observed throughout the society "from top to bottom." With complete disregard for the subtler interpretations of "socialist legality" which have at times been pressed into service by the party to justify all manner of illegalities, the authors blandly asserted that legality means simply observing the law—always and everywhere.

Although the two scholars escaped censure or attack for this particular article, they did get into trouble as a result of their interventions at a lawyers' congress which took place shortly afterwards (May 1963) in Leningrad. So far as is known, no report of this congress—which was organized by the law faculty of Leningrad University to discuss problems of criminal law—was published, but the nature of the interventions by Professors Ioffe and Shargorodski can be gleaned from the severe attacks made on them in the leading legal periodicals some six months later. The burden of their argument seems to have been that if the observance of legal norms was to become a reality in the USSR, professional academic lawyers must be allowed to offer full and free criticism of legal enactments by the government. Professor Shargorodski was quoted in one of the articles as having said that legal science could only claim to be a science if it had the right to say "no" to practice. One of the objects of his criticism was a decree of the RSFSR of May 6, 1963, increasing the penalty for feeding bread to cattle. A glance at the decree is sufficient to show what prompted Professor Shargorodski's objection. It provides for a fine imposed administratively by the local soviet for a first offense, and only a second offense is made subject to court trial, with conviction entailing a penalty of up to three years imprisonment in addition to confiscation of the offender's cattle. Clearly, therefore, conviction of a second offense, even if decided after proper judicial trial, could well be based on the previous administrative penalization, against which no judicial safeguards are provided and which is therefore open to all manner of procedural abuses.

The two professors were also criticized for urging the desirability of adopting certain principles of bourgeois criminal law and procedure. Reading between the lines, it is plain that what they had argued was that observance of legal norms must prevail over expediency in government legislation and administration. This is presumably what their official critics meant when they wrote that some legal scholars had "incorrectly understood the role of legal science in the solution of the practical tasks of government." But the real trouble seems to have been that these scholars understood it only too well—and were courageous enough to speak their minds.

It must be obvious to any informed student of Soviet society that the prospects for the rule of law in the USSR are not to be overestimated. True, the most recent signs have not been too discouraging: Gorkin's article is a case in point, and the reported releases of both Brodsky and Madame Ivinskaia, if true, would appear to suggest that the new rulers are at least more sensitive than their predecessors to outside civilized opinion regarding such miscarriages of Soviet justice. But one swallow does not make a summer. There is a long tradition of lawlessness and arbitrariness to overcome; a respected and independent judiciary and bar remain to be built up; and the party will have to learn to recognize that when academic lawyers criticize some of the more flagrantly illegal Soviet practices, they do so as loyal Soviet partiots with the best interest of their country at heart. Above all, the party will have to learn to live and act within the law, rather than above it as at present.

This said, there are nonetheless some grounds for moderate optimism. One is that the voice of civilized criticism is now being heard, as indeed it has been continuously since 1953. This is a big change. In Soviet conditions, the fact that criticism is allowed to appear at all leads to the reasonable inference that there are persons in authority who sympathize with the critics—here again, perhaps the Gorkin article may be a case in point. Professors Shargorodski and Ioffe, it is true, have not been allowed to publish since 1963, but one presumes that nothing worse has happened to them (Who would have dared to presume this twelve years ago?), and one can reasonably hope that their works will again appear in the learned journals before long. Slowly, even if very slowly, the responsible Soviet public is learning from these persistent exponents of the rule of law just how the things that are wrong in Soviet legal practice could be put right. This is perhaps the first necessary step towards improvement.

However, the main obstacle to the development of the rule of law is, as it always has been, the vested interest of the party apparatus in arbitrary illegality. This has to some extent been dictated by Soviet conditions of administration. The administrative machine is over-complex, over-centralized, over-bureaucratized, and totally unfit for its task. Only the party can cut through the jungle of administrative red tape, and it has always done so by ignoring the law. Add to this the heritage of several generations of contempt on the part of the party apparatus for the whole state machine, and the results are not difficult to imagine.

Yet it could be that the climate of opinion in the Soviet Union is moving away from this traditional pattern. Technical progress, efficiency of production, and a society geared to a numerous variety of consumer interests demand regularity, and regularity demands legal norms. In Soviet conditions, only the state machine can supply these legal norms. At present the state machine is more powerful vis-à-vis the party machine than it has been for years, and it may continue in this position so long as the offices of prime minister and party first secretary remain separate. It may, of course, soon lose its advantage to the party should one of the party secretaries, like Stalin and Khrushchev before him, be able to combine both offices in his person. On the other hand, this may not occur, and if not, there is a chance that the influence of the party will decline as the influence of the state machine increases.

Should this happen, the outlook for the rule of law would be correspondingly improved. Constitutional changes might follow, and there might be some institutionalization of legal safeguards in place of the present meaningless declaratory platitudes. Modest as this optimism may seem, it is at all events the first time in Soviet history that it has even become possible to contemplate these possibilities.

JEREMY R. AZRAEL

Is Coercion Withering Away?

Jeremy R. Azrael is Associate Professor of Political Science at the University of Chicago, and has written widely on Soviet affairs. His most recent work is Managerial Power and Soviet Politics *(1966), a study of the Soviet managerial elite and its political influence.*

From Jeremy R. Azrael, "Is Coercion Withering Away?," *Problems of Communism* (November–December, 1962), pp. 9–17. Reprinted by permission of the United States Information Agency.

THERE ARE FEW RESPONSIBLE ANALYSTS of Soviet politics who would deny that the level of coercion in Soviet society has dropped since Stalin's death or who would argue now, as they did formerly, that terror is *the* central attribute of the Soviet political system. At the same time, some analysts go to the extreme of suggesting or implying that coercion has largely given way to persuasion and that it will inevitably recede still further into the background, with the result that the Soviet political system will become libertarian and democratic in the relatively near future. While this latter view is far from dominant, it has been disseminated on a wide enough scale to warrant rigorous examination.

Ideally, such an examination should take the form of a systematic study of all of the aspects and dimensions of coercion in the Soviet political system. In these few pages, however, the focus must be limited to aspects of coercion which seem clearly to contravene the principles of constitutional democracy and the standards ordinarily observed in constitutional-democratic politics. Although concrete evidence on this subject is scarce, what evidence is available is sufficient, in the author's judgment, to suggest the need to discount heavily the more sanguine claims and predictions now being aired.

The most graphic institutional expression of the decline in the level of coercion since Stalin's death is the downgrading of the secret police. Today the secret police no longer constitutes a state within a state. It has lost its "private" economic empire and has been subjected to firm party control. However, while its potential as an independent power base has been greatly impaired, the secret police remains an important *instrument* of rule, and one whose prestige and authority Stalin's heirs have been careful to maintain. Even at the 20th Party Congress in February 1956, Khrushchev expressed his concern lest revelation of the incredible abuses perpetrated by the secret police impede the latter's efficiency. He warned that the "distrust of the workers of the state security organs" shown by "some comrades" was "incorrect and harmful" and announced that the task of the party was "to strengthen the state security agencies in every way." At the 21st Congress in 1959, he spoke of the need "to consolidate the state security organs" and characterized as "stupid and criminal" suggestions that they be weakened.

Role of the Secret Police

Statements of this sort (many others could be cited) should serve as a caution against exaggerating the degree to which the secret police has been emasculated. Now, as under Stalin, every sizable plant, farm, military unit, office, and higher school has its own *spetsodel* (special department). The regime still attempts to imbue the population with the conviction that nothing of political significance escapes the attention of the secret police, and there is every reason to believe that the latter continues to maintain an extensive network of informers and to keep dossiers on a considerable segment of the population. The Soviet leaders, it is true, claim that today the primary function of the secret police is to thwart foreign espionage, but this does not in any sense imply that the secret police is limited to ordinary counter-intelligence activities. Soviet security-consciousness is such that immense areas of life are "classified," and Soviet suspiciousness is such that almost all forms of deviant behavior are seen as signs of potential footholds for capitalist subversion. Indeed, one important article on the need for "vigilance" argues that even exemplary behavior is no proof of loyalty, warning that "it is difficult to recognize *the hidden enemy* . . . [who] is usually disguised as an honest Soviet man, even as a patriot and activist." Here we find the ultimate in terroristic logic, the position that everyone in the society is suspect. . . .

Political Crimes

At the 21st Party Congress, Khrushchev claimed that "at the present time there are no instances of people being brought to trial for political crimes (*za politicheskiie prestupleniia*)." In appraising this claim one is entitled, at a minimum, to presume bad faith on Khrushchev's part. On the very eve of the Congress, the Supreme Soviet approved a new "law on state crimes" which added "conspiracy to seize power" to the list of acts defined as treasonable, in what was clearly an effort to pave the way for the prosecution of the so-called "anti-party group." The fact that none of the members of the "anti-party group" has been prosecuted is more a consequence of high-level politics than of judicial policy and does nothing to mitigate the hypocrisy of Khrushchev's claim—unless one takes the phrase "at the present moment" literally, which makes the statement merely ridiculous.

As is well known, the early phases of the succession struggle after Stalin's death witnessed a number of executions for "political crimes," and as late as 1957 Khrushchev admitted to an American journalist that trials for "political crimes" were still taking place, claiming only that "political crimes have become *'rarities'* " and that "of those deservedly punished for anti-Soviet activities in recent years, *most* are agents sent into the Soviet Union from abroad." Furthermore, trials for "political crimes" continued after the 21st Congress. Leaving aside the trials of "agents sent from abroad," there are cases on record of convictions for "especially dangerous state crimes" committed by "Nazi collaborators" (generally brought to trial under the totalitarian formula—"In view of the especially serious nature of the crimes the court decided to suspend the statute of limitations") by pacifists (guilty of "anti-Soviet agitation and propaganda"), and by unsuccessful defectors (flight abroad being defined as *treason* in the USSR). In addition, reliable Soviet informants have reported that sentences of seven years' imprisonment have been imposed on people possessing unauthorized Western literature (such as the *New York Times*), and that as of May 1962 prosecutions have been resumed for the telling of "political" jokes. In both instances the charges involve the "especially dangerous state crime" of possessing materials for, or engaging in, "anti-Soviet agitation and propaganda.". . .

There is no reason to believe that such cases are isolated or atypical. Soviet law and judicial policy may be less of a mockery than they were under Stalin, but it remains true—as the preamble to the new law on "state crimes" makes clear—that they are still based "on the need for *the greatest possible* defense of . . . [the] state." Indeed, Soviet jurists are still disputing the very legitimacy of recognizing defense of the rights of citizens as one of the functions of law.

Ius Populi—Soviet Style

If Soviet law as enforced by the police and administered by the courts falls far short of constitutional-democratic standards of legality, this is even more true of Soviet law as enforced and administered by the so-called "public organizations"—the "comrades' courts," "voluntary brigades," and "public meetings," recently endowed by the regime with quasi-police and quasi-judicial functions. The broadening of the function of the "public organizations" has been heralded by the Soviets and some Westerners as a sign of increasing "democratization." However, this view is untenable if one takes democracy to mean more than mass participation. The "public organizations" are in no sense autonomous bodies but are merely "transmission belts" functioning under the firm control of the central authorities. The Soviet regime has always sought to manipulate group pressure for its own ends and to use the *kollektiv* to reinforce and supplement formal governmental coercion. The "public organizations," viewed in this perspective, simply represent a further stage in the institutionalization of group pressures.

It is the strengthening of the "public organizations" that forms the basis of Soviet claims of achieving a transition from "punitive" to "prophylactic" coercion. The distinction, as we shall see, is often meaningless—*e.g.,* the "anti-parasite" laws are depicted as "prophylactic" in character. But even where there is a distinction, what is involved in "prophylaxis" is not a relaxation of pressure but a fundamental assault on all aspects of privacy, including those which are not formally prescribed by law. In sum, the "public organizations" do not represent "democratization" in any meaningful sense, but rather a simultaneous effort on the regime's part to increase its ideological legitimacy, to remove from its own shoulders the immediate onus for coercive measures, to force more and more citizens to become its active accomplices, and to extend its range of effective control. . . .

Coercion: Direct and Indirect

Thus far we have discussed political coercion with reference to the operations of its major instruments: of the secret police, the courts, and the "public organizations." In conclusion, it is necessary to take note of phenomena which, while less directly associated with specific agencies of coercion, are nonetheless immensely relevant to the subject of this article.

Perhaps the broadest application of coercion since Stalin's death has occurred in conjunction with the settlement of the Virgin Lands.[1] There is no doubt that many of the well over one million "volunteers" who have journeyed to Siberia and Kazakhstan did so unwillingly. The very vocabulary which the Soviets use is indicative. People rarely "go" to the Virgin Lands; they are always "allocated," "dispatched," or "sent"—of course, on a "voluntary" basis. At a minimum, "volunteers" are enlisted at open public meetings in an atmosphere of artificially generated enthusiasm. Regularly, appeals for "volunteers" are accompanied

---

[1] The Virgin Lands program has since been liquidated. The point remains valid, however, since Soviet youth continue to be conscripted for other types of summer projects related to economic production. [Editor's note.]

by warnings that those who hold back will be looked upon as "idlers" and "shirkers" of doubtful commitment and loyalty to the Communist cause. Where students have been solicited to aid in summer harvesting, failure to "volunteer" has regularly been followed by expulsion from the Komsomol and university. The prevailing climate is suggested by one of the author's own experiences when he expressed his sympathy to a young Soviet friend who had broken his leg. The friend replied, "Oh, it's not really so bad, at least I can get a medical release from this year's Virgin Land detail." In this connection, it is worth noting that (according to *Komsomolskaia pravda*) at Leningrad University even those with medical releases were treated as "malingerers" and "deserters."

Another realm in which coercion has been broadly applied is that of the peasants' private homes, plots and herds. In conjunction with the movement to merge collective farms (and/or transform them into state farms), many peasants have been forced to evacuate their homes and move into new, consolidated village centers. That this resettlement has always, or even often, been voluntary is doubtful; indeed, if rumor in Moscow is to be believed, it has regularly been accomplished by brute force, complete with the razing of old homesteads. Also, in a good many cases, the regime's campaign to transfer all privately-owned cows to the collective farms has involved the use of force and violence. Thus, *Pravda* reported in 1958 that *kolkhoz* chairmen in a number of raions in the Ukraine were "compelling *kolkhozniks* to transfer privately-owned cattle to the common herds under guise of purchase." That this practice has continued despite *Pravda's* criticism has been borne out by Khrushchev himself, who at a February 1961 meeting with Ukrainian agricultural officials criticized "people who compel the collective farmers to sell their cows." It is difficult to imagine that the "people" whom Khrushchev had in mind engaged in this practice entirely on their own initiative: more likely, in responding to central directives, they *overreacted*, and then were used as scapegoats in traditional Soviet style (shades of "Dizzy With Success"!). The transfer of cows goes on— as does the regime's program of transferring all private plots to the collectives. The latter is an extremely sensitive issue, and the authorities have been proceeding with great caution. However, it is proceeding, most likely to the accompaniment of coercion—an assumption which is grounded in everything we know about Soviet peasant attitudes.

Finally, brief mention should be made of what might be called *latent* coercion—that is, coercion in the form of *threats*. Even a random sampling of the relevant sources is enough to demonstrate the continued prevalence of this particular form of political coercion. To some extent this may signify nothing more than a sort of rhetorical residue of Stalinism. However, the rulers of the Soviet Union do not ordinarily choose their words lightly, and there can be little doubt that they look upon threats as important weapons.

The most conspicuous threats in recent years have been directed, of course, against the "anti-party group," which has been denounced as an "anti-people group" (recalling Stalin's phrase "enemy of the people"), a "real conspiracy against the party," and a clique intending to "decapitate the party leadership." Less conspicuous but no less ominous threats have been directed at party and executive cadres, as a warning, no doubt, not to take the campaign against the "anti-party group" as a further step in "de-Stalinization" and hence, in some respects, a pledge to abstain from Stalin-like practices. Similarly, economic officials have been warned that certain kinds of failures and "deviations" in industry and agriculture may be treated as "political crimes." This is the clear import, for example, of Khrushchev's warnings to agricultural officials who engaged in practices in which "only enemies of the socialist state" could engage. The same applies to his statement at the 21st Congress that it was necessary to replace those officials who "because of age or for other reasons can no longer carry out with the necessary energy and active spirit the work entrusted to them." True, Khrushchev went on to state that "in the majority of cases they are good comrades, loyal to the party," but, while a relatively sanguine outsider might consider this last sentence conciliatory, almost a guarantee against political coercion, to an *apparatchik* or manager the crucial question may be how to avoid being numbered among the *minority* which is *not* considered loyal to the party.

Another group which has been the object of constant threats is the cultural intelligentsia. At his famous meetings with writers and artists in 1957, Khrushchev interlarded his pleas for a voluntary restoration of discipline with a heavy admixture of threats, including, it is alleged on good authority, a promise that in the event of continued dissidence "our hand will not tremble." In 1960, at another meeting with members of the intelligentsia, Khrushchev went out of his way to cite the case of three young institute staff members who had been expelled from the party for "anti-party activities"; after disclosing that he had rejected an appeal on their behalf by a prominent academician, he went on to warn those concerned that if they "did not understand the stern warning given them, more serious measures would be used against them." Characteristically, the metaphor he chose to depict the party's relation to the writers was that of a forester who periodically has to thin the forest in order to maintain its general health. More recently an even more ominous note has been sounded by Shelepin, who lashed out against certain "unstable elements" among the cultural intelligentsia, accusing them of engaging in "sabotage on the ideological front."

Many more examples of threats could be cited if space permitted. But only two more general points about the role of threats in Soviet society need be noted. First, thanks to the lingering memory of Stalinism, the present regime can count on its threats being taken in earnest even when they are only irregularly implemented. Actually, threats are more regularly implemented than is commonly realized. To take the case of the cultural intelligentsia, for every Yevtushenko who enjoys apparent immunity, there are many others whose "deviations" *are* punished. . . .

Hallmark of Totalitarianism

The second thing to be noted is that quite apart from their immediate content and direction and quite apart from their role in forestalling or inducing specific actions by specific individuals and groups, threats serve to create an atmosphere of intimidation, if not of terror, which inhibits the growth of unauthorized ties of solidarity and of a spirit of "normalcy," trust, and confidence. Here, too, memory plays a key role, leading many people to exaggerate the intensity of threats and to assume that they are intended to apply broadly rather than narrowly even when this is not the case. However, as the vagueness of the categories of action and attitude which are the target of threats indicates, this indeed is very often the case.

The main purpose of the preceding pages has been to delineate some of the major dimensions of political coercion in the Soviet Union today. As noted at the outset, the evidence is too scanty and ambiguous to permit firm conclusions or far-reaching generalizations. However, it is certainly adequate to show that the role of coercion is much greater in the Soviet Union than in democratic countries, and to demonstrate the inappropriateness of references to the USSR as a society in which "people are no longer scared of the police," or as one characterized by a "new reign of law." Nor does the evidence lend much support to the notion that references of this sort are merely "slightly premature." It is worth noting that the evidence points to a *rise* in the level of coercion since the 21st Party Congress. The fact that this was the first congress to meet after the succession struggle had been resolved (by the rout of the "anti-party group") suggests that the decrease in coercion which followed Stalin's death was partly due to tactical considerations on the part of those participating in the struggle for power, and that it was merely of temporary significance. At the same time, the rise in the level of coercion seems less likely to be short-lived, because it is intimately related to Khrushchev's effort to revitalize Bolshevik ideology and his programmatic commitment to the realization of what is called full-fledged communism. . . .

Though it has risen in recent years, the level of coercion in Soviet society has certainly not reached Stalinist heights. That it could not do so is far from clear. Many have argued that social and economic developments make a "return to Stalinism" impossible, but there is good reason to remain skeptical. The arguments are too complex to be treated here and have in any case received considerable attention elsewhere; but surely the example of Nazi Germany suffices to suggest that neither a high degree of "industrial maturity" nor an eminently educated population are guarantees against a terroristic political system—quite apart from the fact that in Russia, as Khrushchev's successful implementation of major programs opposed by key professional and managerial groups indicates, the powers of resistance of the Soviet "new class" are very slight indeed. Certainly there are no *institutional* barriers against a "return to Stalinism." The Procurator-General of the USSR has argued that the Soviet constitution and legal system provide "reliable guarantees" against a reversion to Stalinism, but one has only to recall the sundry "guarantees" in the so-called "Stalinist Constitution" (still in force to this day) to realize how specious this argument is. Police Chief Shelepin was perhaps more realistic when he assured the 21st Congress that "this shameful business . . . will never be repeated" *because* "the party and the Central Committee will never allow it." The desire of the leadership is now and will be for some time to come *the* key factor determining the level of coercion in Soviet society.

We have seen that, having consolidated its position, the leadership has increased the level of coercion and shown signs of desiring to increase it still further. However, that it desires or will desire to increase it to Stalinist heights seems unlikely. The reason is not that the present regime is less committed than Stalin to total control, but rather that it is less paranoiac; that it is possessed of more subtle means of control deriving from successful industrialization; and that, thanks in part to the massive indoctrination (intellectual coercion) of the past 45 years, as well as to the relaxation of outright terror, it can count upon a wider acceptance of its policies, even when these policies contribute to the further consolidation of totalitarian rule. The Soviet Union is still very far from a "consensual" or "popular" totalitarianism in which external coercion would be superfluous due to the internalization of totalitarian *mores*. However, it is equally far—indeed farther—from constitutional democracy.

IV Equality and Discrimination in Soviet Society

YAROSLAV BILINSKY

Nationalities and the Ruling Elite

Yaroslav Bilinsky is Associate Professor of Political Science at the University of Delaware. Specializing in nationality problems of the Soviet Union, he is the author of a number of articles on the subject, and of The Second Soviet Republic: The Ukraine After World War II (*1964*).

IN A REPORT published under the auspices of UNESCO five years ago, I. P. Tsamerian and S. L. Ronin described the "general nationality policy of the Soviet state" as designed "to insure the more rapid development of formerly backward nations in all fields," adding that "only such a policy is capable of bringing about genuine equality between all the republics which make up the great land of socialism, the Soviet Union, and between all the peoples and nationalities inhabiting it." Similar enthusiasm for this policy was voiced just last year by T. Usabaliev, the native First Secretary of the Communist Party of Kirghizia. "One of the remarkable results of the development of Soviet Kirghizia," he wrote, "has been the creation of her own national cadres. In our epoch, this constitutes one of the most significant indices of a nation's maturity and the most important condition of its genuine progress."

If these quotations are taken at face value, the central objective of Soviet nationality policy would appear to be to raise the cultural, political, social and economic level of the various minority peoples of the USSR so as to ensure their attainment of "genuine equality" as Soviet citizens. The present article proposes to examine in detail

Excerpted from Yaroslav Bilinsky, "The Rulers and the Ruled," *Problems of Communism* (September-October, 1967), pp. 16–26. Reprinted by permission of the United States Information Agency.

one of the most important criteria of the attainment of this proclaimed objective: namely, the extent of political participation by the diverse nationalities as measured by their representation in the major organs of political rule in the USSR.

The problem of nationality representation has been an extraordinarily complex one for the Soviet Union. The Soviet census of 1959 listed as many as 109 different ethnic groups, 22 of which numbered more than 900,000 members each. Russians constitute a majority in the country as a whole and in the Russian Federative Republic, but they are a minority in the other union republics. The non-Russian peoples, on the other hand, are minorities in the total Soviet population, but virtually all of them (except the Kazakhs and the Kirghiz) constitute majorities in their own native regions, which were conquered by the Russian Tsars at different times, some as late as the second half of the 19th century. To add to the complexity, some of these regions were as much, if not more, advanced economically and socially than the Russian metropolis, while others (*e.g.*, in Central Asia) were inhabited by semi-nomadic tribes. The Jews, who were openly discriminated against under the Tsars, presented a special problem of their own.

Evolution of Nationality Policy

Before 1917, governing power rested in the hands of Russians and a sprinkling of Russified Germans, Ukrainians and others. Much to the credit of the Soviet regime, it explicitly recognized the existence of the nationalities problem, barred antisemitic discrimination (at least during the 1920's), set up formally sovereign union republics for the larger peoples, and went about training indigenous personnel in all walks of life. The less developed the area, the more accelerated was to be the pace of advancement: indigenous cadres were to be produced as quickly as possible and by the thousands. Partly to facilitate this process and partly to appeal to the already existing indigenous intelligentsias, the native languages were introduced as the principal medium of instruction in the rapidly expanding school systems of the non-Russian republics. This was, in essence, the famous policy of *korenizatsiia*—a term sometimes translated as "indigenization"—which was initiated about 1921.

The controlling purpose of this policy was, however, precisely what its name implied: an effort by the central authority to take root in the non-Russian areas. The results soon became apparent. To take Kazakhstan as an example, only 349, or 4.4 percent, of the 8,618 members of the Kazakh Communist Party organization were native Kazakhs at the beginning of 1922, but by January 1, 1937, the proportion of Kazakhs had risen to 48.8 percent. In the middle 1930's, however, the policy of *korenizatsiia* was abandoned. A respectable minimum of indigenous personnel had been trained and placed. At the same time, some of the newly-installed native party leaders began arguing that *korenizatsiia* was a poor substitute for real political and cultural autonomy and started questioning the continued absolute predominance of the central authorities. They were at first eliminated one by one—Sultan Galiev, Khvylovy, Skrypnyk—and then liquidated by the thousands during Stalin's Great Purge. Above all, strict centralization and the utilization of existing cadres from the more advanced nationalities (Russians, Georgians, Armenians, Ukrainians, and Jews) were considered more compatible with centralized planning and rapid industrial-ization than a policy emphasizing the systematic advancement of the less-developed nationalities.

The first seven postwar years saw a trend toward extreme glori-fication of everything Russian, which was heralded by Stalin's well-known toast to the Russian people on May 24, 1945. Although the growth of the native intelligentsia in the non-Russian republics continued, it was less openly favored by the regime, and the emerg-ing *natsionaly* were subjected to heavy pressures for Russification. As for the Jews, Stalin instituted a particularly strident policy of discrimination against them in 1948, and a decision taken in the same year aimed at the destruction of Soviet Jewry as a community.

Stalin's death brought relief to all the non-Russian peoples with the exception of the Jews. In his drive to power between 1953 and 1958, Khrushchev deliberately courted party officials in the outlying republics, where he faced less challenge than in Moscow itself, and this benefited local non-Russian party leaders. Some of them were elevated to responsible positions in Moscow, and at the same time their fellow countrymen in the republics were given greater authority in economic administration and more leeway in cultural policy.

Recent Policy

In mid-1958, however, Khrushchev reversed the more liberal nationalities policy which he himself had instituted. With the defeat of the "anti-party group," the ouster of Zhukov in 1957, and Bulganin's forced resignation in 1958, Khrushchev may have felt that his position was sufficiently consolidated so that he need no longer woo the support of the non-Russian party organizations. At the same time, in the wake of the essentially nationalist-inspired upheavals of 1956 in Poland and Hungary, unrest was beginning to spread to the non-Russian republics of the USSR. One manifestation of this was an attempt by the Latvian party organization to place restrictions on non-Latvian personnel, which led to a wholesale purge of its leadership in mid-1959. Still another factor which influenced the shift in nationalities policy was Khrushchev's decision, spurred by the ideological challenge from Communist China, to accelerate the Soviet advance toward communism. "Building communism" became the slogan of the extraordinary 21st Party Congress in January 1959 and the premise of the new Party Program of 1961. (Though this theme has since been deemphasized somewhat, and the timetable for the attainment of communism extended, the Program still remains binding.)

In the field of nationality relations, this policy has entailed a more pronounced subordination of the interests and aspirations of the individual nationalities to the interests of the Soviet Union and its predominant ethnic group, the Russians. The teaching of Russian in the schools of the non-Russian republics has been pushed despite protests from several of these republics. So has the large-scale immigration of workers and other personnel from the more advanced Soviet republics even though it resulted in lowering the indigenous peoples' share in the population of their own republics. This was justified on the ground that the less advanced non-Russian republics could not develop their own resources without outside help, and also that the exchange of people and cadres would contribute towards a harmonious fusing together of nationalities and thus hasten the advent of communism. That a breakdown of national barriers could result in ethnic inequality and discrimination was admitted only for capitalist countries.

Since Khrushchev's fall, the emphasis on inter-republican exchange of personnel has continued and in the long run may threaten the progress of the less advanced peoples towards autonomy and full political equality. . . .

Access to Key Republican Posts

. . . Let us now see to what extent persons of the titular or indigenous nationality are represented in the key party . . . positions in their own republics. . . . It is apparent to begin with that the party first secretary has been in all cases a person of indigenous nationality, while in most cases the second secretary has not. This is significant, for while the first secretary occupies the formally more prominent position and bears general political responsibility for affairs in his republic, the second secretary is as a rule the person in charge of the *kadry* and as such wields practical control over the entire republican party apparatus. In the Russian, Ukrainian and Belorussian republics, both posts are held by persons of the indigenous nationality, reflecting the favored status of these three Slavic nationalities. The two other exceptions— Estonia and Armenia—are less readily explainable, although in the case of Estonia the explanation may lie in the fact that the party leadership was purged for its excessive nationalism in 1950 and has since been dominated by a "Muscovite faction" made up of Estonians who spent the interwar years in the Soviet Union. In all the remaining ten republics, the second secretary is either a Russian or a Ukrainian, with the Russians predominating (though less so in 1966 than in 1961). Especially striking is the fact that the strong Georgian party, which had a Georgian second secretary from at least early 1949 until August 1956, has since had a Russian occupying that post—probably as a consequence of the disturbances which occurred in Georgia in March 1956 after Khrushchev denounced Stalin. . . .

Representation at the Center

Given the extreme centralization which characterizes the Soviet governing system, the representation of the different nationalities within their own respective union republics, "autonomous republics" or "autonomous regions" is far outweighed in importance by their representation in the central organs of power. It is striking that in the Supreme Soviet—the most representative national body but also the least powerful—the Russians and, to a lesser extent, the Ukrainians and Belorussians are actually underrepresented in relation to their proportions of the total population, while there is an overrepresentation of many of the lesser nationalities such as the Kazakhs, Georgians, Armenians, Azerbaijanis, Kirghiz, Latvians, Estonians, Bashkirs, etc. In large part, this stems from the system of representation in the second chamber of the Supreme Soviet, the Council of Nationalities, where each union republic, regardless of its population, has 32 delegates, each autonomous republic 11, and each autonomous *oblasi* (region) five. In specific cases, other factors may enter in: *e.g.*, the nearly triple overrepresentation of the Georgians may perhaps be explained in part by their proverbial national pride and the fact that, despite their small number, they are among the best-educated national groups in the USSR.

In sharp contrast to the overrepresentation of some of the relatively insignificant nationalities is the approximate one-third underrepresentation of the Jews, who constitute 1.09 percent of the Soviet population while there are only five Jewish deputies in the Supreme Soviet, or only 0.35 percent of its membership. The tiny Abkhazian group of 65,000 (0.03 percent of the total USSR population) sends more deputies (seven) to the Supreme Soviet than do the 2.3 million Soviet Jews. The present low level of Jewish representation, it should be noted, reflects a sharp decrease from as late as 1947, when there were 32 Jewish deputies in the Supreme Soviet. This decline appears to be the result of a deliberate policy initiated by Stalin in 1948, and continued under Khrushchev, of imposing restrictive quotas on the Jews not only in political activity but in other areas as well.

Turning to the Central Committee and the Politburo-Secretariat, we find a single Jew on the Central Committee—V. E. Dymshits, who for all his imposing titles . . . appears to be more of a high-ranking economic technician than a policymaker. We further find the Ukrainians still strongly represented—next to the Russians—on both the Central Committee and the Politburo, although, as explained below, this is no longer true of the Secretariat alone.

The marked influx of Ukrainians into high party positions during the Khrushchev era has already been ably analyzed . . . by Seweryn Bialer, who attributed it to a combination of two factors: Khrushchev's close personal ties with leading members of the Ukrainian party, of which he had once been first secretary, and the inherent importance of the Ukrainian republic (second largest in the USSR) in Soviet politics. This trend appears to have reached its peak with the elevation of Nikolai V. Podgorny, in June 1963, to the Secretariat, where another Ukrainian, Vitali N. Titov, was already a secretary and chairman of the Central Committee's Commission on Party-Organizational Questions, and with the 1964 promotion of P. Ye. Shelest to full membership in the Politburo. Since the accession of the Brezhnev-Kosygin leadership, however, both Titov and Podgorny have been relieved of their Secretariat posts—Titov in April 1965, when he was quietly demoted to second secretary of the Kazakh party; and Podgorny in April 1966, when he was not reelected to the Secretariat so that he might devote himself more fully to his new but largely honorific post as Chairman of the Presidium of the Supreme Soviet. As a result, though they still retain their four-man representation in the Politburo (Podgorny, D. S. Polianski, Shelest, and alternate member V. V. Shcherbitski), the Ukrainians are now completely out of the Secretariat, which consists entirely of Russians.

In contrast to the ebbing political fortunes of the Ukrainians, there has been a notable rise in Belorussian representation in the central party organs since the fall of Khrushchev and the advent of the Brezhnev regime. . . . In the Central Committee elected by the 23rd Congress in April 1966, the Belorussians increased their number of full members to ten as compared with six on the 1961 Central Committee (although there was a drop in the number of alternate members). Moving to the more select Politburo, we now find one Belorussian full member: K. T. Mazurov, who was elevated from candidate to full membership and also made a first deputy chairman of the USSR Council of Ministers in March 1965; and P. M. Masherov, who was elected a candidate member of the Politburo at the 23rd Congress. In 1961, Mazurov had been the only Belorussian on the Politburo, and only as a candidate member; now, as senior first deputy chairman of the Council of Ministers, he outranks his Ukrainian colleague, Polianski, both on the Politburo and in the Soviet government. Masherov's rise to candidate membership on the Politburo was even more remarkable, for he had only become a full member of the Central Committee in November 1964 after having been an alternate since 1961. His promotion to the Politburo in April 1966 was therefore exceptionally fast.

The reasons for the apparent shift of influence from the Ukrainians to the Belorussians are no doubt political. As pointed out earlier, Khrushchev's personal ties with Ukrainian party leaders probably led him to favor them as a means of bolstering his support in the top party organs. On the other hand, Professor Robert M. Slusser, in an article published on the heels of Khrushchev's fall, found evidence to indicate that the opposition to Khrushchev, as early as the 22nd Party Congress in 1961, had deliberately courted the support of the small but solid Belorussian party organization. The somewhat diminished Ukrainian representation in the central party organs and the strengthened position of the Belorussians would thus appear to reflect a settling of political scores by the new regime.

In analyzing the favored position of both the Ukrainians and the Belorussians in the overall nationalities picture in the USSR, it should be borne in mind that these two peoples, together with the Russians, belong to the East Slavic group, and that all three share many cultural traits and historical traditions. The Ukrainians selected by Khrushchev to serve as watchdogs of the central party authorities in some of the Central Asian republics, for example, are doubtless hardly distinguishable from Russians so far as the Kazakhs and Kirghiz are concerned. Similarly, the promotion of Belorussians to influential party posts may be viewed by Brezhnev as a more natural and safer course than the elevation of, say, Armenians or Georgians to positions of authority.

In the USSR Council of Ministers . . . the predominance of Russians is now even more accentuated than in 1962, while the Ukrainian representation has also increased contrary to the trend already noted in the higher party organs. Together, Russians and Ukrainians occupy 64, or 92.8 percent, of the 69 Council posts, with the remaining five positions divided among a scattering of other nationalities. The Belorussians, who were not represented in 1962, now have a single but highly-placed representative by virtue of K. T. Mazurov's 1965 appointment as first deputy chairman of the Council. The lone Jewish member is V. E. Dymshits, who is a deputy chairman and also chairman of the State Committee for Material and Technical Supply. Armenia, formerly represented by First Deputy Chairman Anastas Mikoyan, is now represented by L. A. Kostandov, Minister of Chemical Industry. The single Komi, both in 1962 and 1966, is economist Vladimir N. Starovski, who has headed the Central Statistical Office of the Council of Ministers since 1948, and the newly added Tatar is Fuad B. Yakubovski, Minister of Assembling and Special Construction Work. The last four mentioned certainly are on the Council of Ministers not by virtue of their nationality but because of their special individual expertise in certain areas.

The Quota System—An Assessment

The main burden of this article has been to show the operation of a *limited* nationality-quota system in filling political offices in the USSR. With certain exceptions, seats in the Supreme Soviet are allocated to the various nationalities in rough proportion to their respective numbers in the total Soviet population, but as has been pointed out, this principle tends to be applied more and more restrictively and discriminatorily as one moves to the higher organs of state and party where real power is centered. Within the non-Russian republics themselves, under the recently emphasized policy of interrepublican exchanges of personnel, we find Russians and Ukrainians holding key positions in the republican party organizations. At the center, Russian-Ukrainian predominance has been even more pronounced, with the Belorussians recently coming into increased prominence. The really crucial positions in the party Secretariat, however, are now held exclusively by Russians.

The way in which the nationality-quota system operates poses the moral question of whether it is just to discriminate among citizens of one and the same state on grounds other than ability and merit. Its application to Soviet Jewry in particular makes the question more poignant, for the regime is apparently trying to destroy the Soviet Jews as a group while continuing to discriminate against them as individuals. Soviet morality, however, makes the interests of the state paramount.

How do the lesser nationalities feel about the operation of the quota system? It would seem that the principle of proportional representation would be popular with them insofar as it enables their representatives to attain leading political offices in their own republics, responsible positions in the more "dignified" central organs in Moscow, and at least secondary positions in the more "efficient" organs of central power. That it is definitely a matter of concern to them to be adequately represented not only at the all-Union level but, above all, in their own republics is evident from the following statement made by G. O. Zimanas, a member of the Central Committee of the Lithuanian CP, in an article published last year:

The representatives of any Soviet nation whatsoever judge their rights, including their nationality rights, not only and not so much by what functions their deputies (*poslantsy*) fulfill in the all-Union organizations, but also by what they can actually accomplish themselves in the sphere of administering state and public affairs [in their own republic].

It is precisely the ability of the lesser nationalities to run their own national affairs that is threatened by the new emphasis on the interexchange of responsible personnel between republics. Certainly, the Kazakhs or the Kirghiz cannot be enthusiastic about the immigration into their republics of so-called "elder brothers"—mainly Russians and Ukrainians—to assume important positions in the local party and state administration. To please the smaller peoples, the regime is continuing to train indigenous cadres, but to a more limited extent than in the 1920's and 1930's, and their hopes of advancement would appear to be diminishing under the present policy.

On the other hand, the more socio-economically and culturally advanced but less numerous nationalities, such as the Georgians and Armenians, not to mention the Jews, may very well resent the fact that the operation of the quota system restricts them to all but token representation in the central organs of political authority. The Georgians, who once enjoyed a favored position under Stalin, now find themselves reduced to but two full members and one alternate in the Central Committee and a single member of the Politburo—and they must resent even more the fact that the Georgian CP itself has had a Russian second secretary since 1956. The Armenians, too, cannot be happy over the unceremonious retirement of Anastas Mikoyan from the Politburo, which leaves them without representation there.

The nationalities problem thus remains a difficult and thorny one for the Soviet leaders. As the 50th anniversary of the Communist regime draws near, they must have learned that there is one thing more difficult than conquering an empire—and that is maintaining it.

BOHDAN R. BOCIURKIW

Believers and Non-believers

Bohdan R. Bociurkiw is Associate Professor of Political Science at the University of Alberta, Canada. He has written a number of articles on Soviet affairs, particularly in the area of religion, and is currently preparing a book on Leninism and religion.

Excerpted from Bohdan Bociurkiw, "Religion and Soviet Society," *Survey* (July, 1966), pp. 62–71. Reprinted by permission.

FROM THE VERY INCEPTION of the Soviet regime, its attempts to cope with the problem of religion in the USSR have been hampered by its dogmatic assumptions concerning the nature, roots, and social functions of religion. Derived from Marx and Engels in a rather simplified Leninist version, the Bolshevik notion of religion reduced it to a socially harmful "illusion" born out of men's ignorance and their fear of the natural and social forces controlling their existence. Equated with a "spiritual *sivukha*, in which the slaves of capitalism drown their human image," religion was viewed as a psychological tool used by the exploiters to keep the oppressed classes docile, apathetic, incapable of overthrowing the seemingly providential status quo. In their service the ruling classes employed the greedy clergy who perpetrated "frauds" upon the credulous masses, justifying and sweetening their unhappy lot with the promise of an imaginary happiness in the next world. Not answering any universal human need, not rooted in any eternal religious sentiment, religion was destined to share the fate of the class system, private property, and exploitation. Through a combination of systematic scientific-atheist education and the operation of social economic forces liberated by the proletarian revolution, the toiling masses were to liberate themselves fully from "religious prejudices."

The nearly fifty years of anti-religious struggle and social engineering which were expected to eliminate the "social roots" of religion in the USSR, failed to emancipate the masses from "religious illusion." Since the launching of the first five-year plan, this moment of deliverance has seemed to be just over the horizon, as the Soviet Union evolved through economic and social upheavals, the purges and the war into an increasingly complex industrial and literate society under an apparently all-powerful dictatorship. To be sure, by the end of the thirties *organized* religion had been almost completely suppressed throughout the country, but for all its massive efforts in atheist indoctrination the regime could not destroy religious *beliefs* in a large section of the population. Pragmatist as he was, Stalin drew a lesson from the failure of the anti-religious campaign when the German attack on the USSR made it imperative to mobilize all human and material resources for the country's war effort. Limited concessions were granted to the Russian Orthodox Church and to other religious groups which could be utilized for the purposes of the Kremlin's domestic and foreign policies. Under the new precarious *modus vivendi* between the atheist regime and the "patriotic" religious groups, organized religion has experienced a significant, though partial, revival, and has indeed been recapturing some of the ground it had lost among the younger generation.

In seeking to explain the tenacity of "religious survivals" in the post-war USSR, Soviet theoreticians have not only been constrained by the narrow Leninist frame of reference but were also compelled to maintain the fiction that with the construction of socialism such sources of "religious illusion" as fear, insecurity, dependence, exploitation and alienation, had been eliminated in Soviet society. Consequently, they have found it necessary to fall back on such rationalizations as "ideological lag," "external capitalist influence," "the war," and, above all, the "neglect" or "inadequacy of anti-religious propaganda" and the persistent "activities of churchmen and sectarians." However, as the post-Stalin thaw slightly relaxed the dogmatic framework of Soviet philosophy, cautious voices began to appear in scholarly exchanges, criticizing the limitations of the official view of religious phenomena in Soviet society.

The most serious challenge appeared in an article by P. P. Cherkashin published by *Voprosy filosofii* in June 1958, in which the author asserted the continued existence in the USSR of certain epistemological and social roots of religion. The epistemological base of religion, he suggested, will remain under communism as well, as it derives from the inescapable contradictions "between the attained relative truth and absolute knowledge, between the objective content and the subjective form, between direct, emotional contemplation and the abstract logical work of the mind." The vitality of religious survivals in the USSR, wrote Cherkashin, must also be explained by certain shortcomings in socialist society—its inequality in rewards, its marginal injustice and coercion.

Real contradictions and difficulties of our society may painfully affect the fate of an individual person, especially one not firmly tied to the collective. . . . In our circumstances, there may be "failures" and "fortunates" not only in family life. Personal plans may be drastically changed or shattered by unforeseen circumstances, unexpected events in the life of the country, some shift or other in economics or politics, not to mention the war. . . .

Moreover, Cherkashin pointed out, religious survivals feed on "certain features of our life" which "simply contradict" socialist principles. Among such features he listed "errors in the direction of agriculture, which were absolutely unnecessary in the history of our society," a seemingly all-powerful bureaucratism with its "isolation from the masses, disregard of their needs and interests," and, in the past, the excesses of Stalinism with its "most crude violations of socialist legality." Finally, Cherkashin notes that Soviet society, especially the rural population, "has not yet fully overcome the dependence of man's activities on the play of elemental natural forces," which also contributes to the survival and revival of religious sentiments among the people.

This attempt to reduce the dogmatic element in the official notion of religion, while carefully confined to the Marxist frame of analysis (criticism of religion is a criticism of society begetting religion), concealed broader implications for Soviet religious policy. As the latter soon took a sharp leftward turn, his article came under attack from the party central committee in July 1959 for its "incorrect conclusion that the very same reasons which nourish religious prejudices in capitalist countries operate also in a socialist society." Shortly afterwards, a *Pravda* editorial (August 21, 1959) restated in familiar terms the official interpretation of the reasons for the continued existence of religious survivals, stressing in particular such "subjective" factors as the weakening of anti-religious propaganda, machinations, and violations of Soviet law by the "servants of religion," and the "laxity of organizations called upon to supervise the strict observance of Soviet legislation on religious cults."

The increasingly violent anti-religious campaign extending from 1959 to 1964 and aimed at the "final and complete uprooting of religious prejudices" in Soviet society, represented a major test of the regime's thinking on religion. On the surface, it produced results which could hardly fail to impress the party's ideological high priests. The number of registered religious congregations in the USSR had been reduced by at least one half of the 1954 total; some denominations, in particular Judaism, lost most of their legal facilities for worship. Of the eight Orthodox theological seminaries reopened since the war, only three survived by 1965 with a greatly reduced enrollment. At least two-thirds of the Orthodox monastic institutions had been closed. Under new laws and regulations severely curtailing the scope of ecclesiastical activities and discouraging laymen from openly performing religious rites, the number of church baptisms, marriages, and funerals had been drastically reduced, especially in large cities. "New Soviet rites" were said to have displaced church feasts and rituals for all but the most "backward" elements of the toilers. In time-honored fashion these fruits of administrative repression were now advertised as the "inevitable" effect of "objective" forces at work in Soviet society.

Since Khrushchev's fall the self-congratulatory mood characteristic of the early 1960's has slowly been displaced by a critical reappraisal of the situation on the "anti-religious front." Apart from the harm it had done to the Soviet image abroad, the "assault on heaven" was found to have hardly reduced the number of believers in the country. Deprived of legal facilities for worship, the embittered faithful have been increasingly resorting to underground religious practices or replenishing the prohibited religious groups. For the authorities, this has magnified the problem of policing religious activities, reviving the specter of a religious underground evolving into a center of active political opposition to the regime. Religious persecution served to intensify eschatological tendencies among the believers, alienating the more fundamentalist, more aggressive, and, significantly, the younger elements from their submissive leaders suspected of "selling out" to the Godless authorities. As for the much publicized *oktiabriny,* "Komsomol weddings," "civil funerals," "consecrations into workers," etc., these synthetic new rites admittedly failed to match the popular appeal, the emotional and aesthetic qualities of the religious ceremonies they were supposed to replace; and the few and far between "Palaces of Happiness" seem to show little improvement upon the bureaucratic routine of the *Zags* offices.

Symptomatic of the new self-critical mood in official circles has been a post mortem on the Khrushchevite anti-religious campaign conducted in the pages of the chief atheist journal *Nauka i religiia,* and in *Komsomolskaia pravda.* Correspondence in the former publication admitted the self-defeating nature of vulgar misrepresentations of religion, concentration on priestly "frauds" and "immorality," insults to believers, and the widespread reliance on intimidation and coercion in closing churches and dissolving religious congregations. "There can be no doubt," admitted a Minsk lecturer, V. Ivanov, "that the violations of the legislation on cults [by the atheists] and the offending of religious sentiments of the believers contribute to the existence of religious survivals." "We must all firmly assimilate one truth," declared a journalist, M. Morozov, that "in their great majority the believers in our country are honest Soviet men, toilers just as we atheists are, and one should treat them with respect." By far the most significant contribution to this discussion had come from a Lvov atheist, G. Kelt. Writing in *Komsomolskaia pravda* (August 15, 1965), she reminded her fellow *antireligiozniki* that religion "cannot be abolished in one day," as it is not "an idle invention" but represents "a historical phenomenon which has existed over thousands of years."

And today we are again lulling ourselves: "many believers in our country had left the church and religion." This is self-deception. One thing is true, that in the greater part of the territory of the Soviet Union there are no churches and no servants of religion. But there are believers. If not Orthodox, then sectarians of all possible shades. . . . The closing of a parish does not make atheists out of the believers. On the contrary, it intensifies the people's attraction towards religion and, in addition, embitters their hearts.

The writer concluded that "a naked, purely negative, bookish-oratorical atheism" would not succeed unless it countered religion at the aesthetic and emotional levels as well. What is needed, she suggested, is a substitute for the church, "a ritual center," a "shrine dedicated to the apotheosis of the genius of Man" combined with a "new ritual that would replace church liturgy."

After a realistic diagnosis of the shortcomings of the campaign, the proposed cure with its Feuerbachian flavor and echoes of *Bogostroitelstvo* appears to have a distinct air of unreality about it. Apart from missing the importance of religious transcendentalism, it seems to misjudge the nature of Soviet society which, despite the party's repeated reindoctrination drives, had been growing increasingly secular, at least in the ideological sense. The combined effect of the contradictions between the official theory and practice, of the bureaucratization of the system and the *Verbürgerlichung* of the Soviet elite, of the rising level of education and sophistication, has been the progressive erosion of the political myth, its substitution by a routinized public ritual and holiday rhetorics. Not the least important reason for the failure of the recent atheist campaign was its inability to overcome the indifference among the party and Komsomol rank and file to the cause of anti-religious struggle. The prevailing view appears to be that religious survivals are common only among the older generation or the less enlightened stratum of the population, that they do not pose any real threat to the regime and society, and that they would eventually fade away in the process of social and economic change, while a militant anti-religious campaign would rather arrest if not actually reverse this process. Significantly, a poll conducted in 1961 by *Komsomolskaia pravda's* Institute of Public Opinion revealed that the majority of the Soviet youth consider adherence to religion among the least of "social evils." Many industrial workers tend to agree with the believers' argument that their religious convictions are a private matter which must not be held against them in the allocation of jobs and benefits. Indeed, among the Soviet intelligentsia—a social stratum least represented among the overt believers—professional *antireligiozniki* have recruited remarkably few collaborators, while gaining the reputation of "a sort of an atheist sect," which had "assimilated from its opponent the worst features of intolerance and fanaticism."

The decline in militant atheism within the politically vocal strata of the Soviet population cannot be dissociated from changes in the overt attitudes of religious organizations towards the regime. Since the 1920's, after the period of open conflict and unsuccessful attempts to secure an equitable compromise with the regime, the Russian Orthodox Church and most other religious groups not only had to pledge their loyalty to the new system but also to accept far-reaching governmental control over their activities and give unconditional support to Soviet policies. Though it was not until the crisis of the last war that the Kremlin saw fit to acknowledge the "patriotic attitude" of religious groups, ever since the late twenties they have been conspicuously loyal, to the extent indeed of endorsing the regime's manifestly false claim that it had never persecuted religion or clergy but only "criminals hiding behind the cloak of religion." In nearly every religious group there were some who found the political and moral price of legality too high, and rather than compromise chose to withdraw into the religious underground; some simply discontinued church attendance and participation in religious rites performed by "legal" clergy.

Changes in the sphere of organized religion in the USSR are not confined to the realm of church-state relations. The institutional power of religion and the scope of religious activities drastically declined under the combined impact of a hostile political environment and social change. The most dramatic change in fortunes was that of the Russian Orthodox Church. The range of ecclesiastic activities was reduced to little more than worship and the administration of rites within the walls of the church.

The Church's revival since the war has been strictly controlled and restricted in line with considerations of political expediency. Neither the total number of open Orthodox churches (which declined from some 15,000 in 1948 to 11,000 in 1961, and may now be fewer than 8,000) nor their geographical distribution are indicative of the actual strength or local density of Orthodox believers. An examination of the "geography" of the Orthodox Church in the USSR shows that the ratio of active churches to the population decreases sharply as one moves from west to east. The most "churchly" areas are those annexed to the USSR since the last war, followed by the territories which experienced a resurgence of religious life under enemy occupation, and the provinces which were threatened by the Germans (and where the Soviet authorities were prepared to grant some concessions to believers); the least "churchly" areas lie beyond the Urals. It is worth noting in this connection that in 1961 the *majority* of all active Orthodox churches and monasteries were located in the Ukrainian SSR (containing only 20 per cent of the total population) and that the Republic's three formerly Uniate *oblasti* (Lvov, Ternopol, Ivano-Frankivsk—2 percent of the total population), accounted then for some 20 percent of all Orthodox churches operating in the USSR.

Some light on the changes in the denominational structure and social base of organized religion has been shed by field research conducted during 1959-62 by Academy of Sciences teams in four, predominantly agrarian, Central Russian *oblasti*—Voronezh, Lipetsk, Riazan, and Tambov—which largely escaped German occupation, with its stimulating effect on organized religion. Some information has also been published on the adjoining Penza oblast.

The Russian Orthodox Church has remained by far the largest (and, *politically*, best adapted) religious group in the country, but much of its present institutional strength derives from the annexation of the Orthodox churches in the new Soviet territories in the west, as well as from the forcible conversion of the Uniates in the Western Ukraine. On the other hand, the Moscow Patriarchate has lost some of the faithful to the underground "Truly Orthodox Christians" and its flock has been persistently raided by the Baptists and other "Western" sects. The Old Believers and such old native sects as the Dukhobors, Molokane, Subbotniki, Malevantsy, Izrailitiane (Old and New), Khlysty and Skoptsy—have been rapidly declining in strength. In contrast, the newer sects of western origin—the Evangelical Christian-Baptists, the Adventists, as well as the banned Pentecostal and Jehovah's Witnesses, have been enlarging their following. While the locus of Orthodoxy's organized strength shifted to the countryside, the "Western" sects have developed a strong urban base, invading some newly industrialized areas only weakly covered by the Orthodox organization. Among the sects, the Baptists appear to be the strongest and most dynamic group; it has the advantage of a less institutionalized structure (which made it less vulnerable to Soviet restrictions and pressures), and has successfully combined an intense missionary zeal with considerable ingenuity in adapting its message and style of operation to the changing social environment. The old sects of Russian origin were on the whole unable to adapt themselves to the new conditions; their withdrawal from the world into closed, self-sufficient communes had become impossible in the thirties with the collectivization of agriculture and the increasingly totalitarian nature of the regime.

After almost half a century of exclusion from public life and school, of the banning of religious instruction of young people under eighteen, and of administrative discrimination against known believers in all walks of Soviet life, all religious groups have been facing for years the specter of their gradual "withering away" in the absence of a large influx of young believers. Indeed, according to a 1963 official estimate, approximately 70 percent of overt believers were then over forty years of age. The average age of members of religious congregations in the USSR varies considerably, however, in different regions (in the newer Soviet territories the age structure of believers comes closer to that of the general population) and among the different denominations. While the published Soviet data are largely incomparable and restricted to sectarian groups only, they suggest that the Old Believers and the native Russian sects have been on the whole far less successful in rejuvenating their ranks than the Western sects. Thus, for example, among new members joining the Evangelical Christian-Baptists in a series of urban centers, nearly one-third were young people. Surprisingly, the youngest membership recorded for any religious congregation belonged to an illegal congregation of the "Truly Orthodox Christians" in the early fifties. Little information is available on the age composition of the Orthodox believers. Observations conducted in the Penza oblast in 1963 revealed that over three-fourths of the regular church-goers consisted of the over-forty age group, though at the 1963 Easter service in Penza approximately one-third of the congregation were identified as children and youth.

Undoubtedly the females (who accounted in 1959 for 55 percent of the total population) constitute a large majority of overt believers. A 1961 estimate placed the proportion of women in religious congregations at about 70 percent. In Orthodox churches some of the auxiliary functions once reserved only for men have now been opened to women. In terms of their educational and occupational characteristics, members of religious groups seem to come primarily from the less educated strata of Soviet society. Apart, again, from the new western *oblasti*, such overlapping categories as housewives, peasants, unskilled workers, and those over working age represent the overwhelming majority of the registered sect members and regular church-goers.

The official interpretation of the composition of religious congregations has persistently stressed the causal relationship between "religious superstitions" and the low levels of education and skill, seclusion from the collective productive process, and limited access to the communication and artistic media. Inevitably, it is claimed, as the general level of education rises, as women are liberated from drudgery and alienation and drawn into the productive collective, as the uses of leisure become more organized and cultured—religion will gradually lose its hold on the less politically mature strata of the population. Apart from some success attained by individual religious groups in recruiting younger (and usually better educated) members, the influx into the ranks of religious congregations of pensioners tends to upset such a simple correlation. Including people of professional and white-collar worker backgrounds, pensioners have come to play an increasingly important role in the administration of local congregations. Thus in the Penza oblast, of 681 members of Orthodox groups in 1962, 225 were pensioners of whom 144 had previously been decorated with orders and medals. Idleness and age alone do not seem a sufficient explanation for this. One must also take into account the relative invulnerability of individuals once they have retired from posts which are as a rule closed to known believers; hence the temptation to reactivate one's beliefs at this stage.

This brings us to the question of the actual spread and intensity of religious beliefs in Soviet society. No one knows for sure how many believers there are in the USSR. Apart from the alleged findings of the abortive 1937 census, no relevant statistical data have been collected and the occasional local polls conducted by Soviet institutions suffer from the understandable reluctance of the unknown proportion of believers to identify themselves as such.

One, however imperfect, index of the extent of religious sentiments in society has been the degree to which births, marriages, and deaths have been accompanied by the corresponding religious rites. The published data for the Riazan and Penza *oblasti*, while restricted to the Orthodox rite, suggest that a much greater proportion of the population resorts to these rites than has usually been asserted by Soviet spokesmen. That large numbers of young people are clearly involved in these practices—in spite of the shortage of churches and clergy and the virtual impossibility of escaping official detection—also tends to show that the common association of religion with old age may not correctly reflect the real situation. Thus in the Riazan oblast, where of the pre-revolutionary total of 991 churches only 61 were operating in 1960 (i.e. one church for 24,000 inhabitants), 60 percent of all children born in 1960 were baptized in church; in the same year, 15 percent of all marriages and 30 percent of all funerals were performed according to the Orthodox rite. In the Penza oblast, in which only 34 churches (against 924 before 1917) remained open in 1962 (one church for 44,000 inhabitants), the corresponding figures for church baptisms, marriages, and funerals were 48.5, 6.4, and 20.9 percent respectively.

While such widespread resort to religious ceremonies, along with the retention of icons in the majority of households investigated, was officially ascribed to pressure and even threats on the part of "fanatical" grandparents, the important fact remains that rather than submit to powerful anti-religious pressures from outside and fight ideological battles at home, many young people place family loyalty above ideological principle. The survival of the family despite all attempts to transform it into another lever of control, has probably been the major factor in ensuring a considerable degree of continuity of religious beliefs and practices in Soviet society. Notwithstanding their exposure to heavy doses of anti-religious propaganda in school, youth organizations, and the army, many young adults in today's USSR are evidently willing not only to tolerate "religious survivals" among the older generation but also to charge their believing grandparents with the care and upbringing of the youngest generation of Soviet citizens.

By all accounts, organized religion in contemporary Soviet society represents only the visible and politically least vulnerable part of a much larger body of actual believers. These appear in varying percentages in all social strata and age groups and range from those totally devoted and prepared to bear witness to their faith, to the "utilitarian believers" careful to light the proverbial candles to both God and Devil. The majority of those born since the 1917 revolution (especially in urban areas) are probably indifferent to religion, but have by no means become converts to militant atheism. While greater urbanization will probably bring a further decline in the number of believers in the USSR, it would seem that as Soviet society comes of age, as it begins to shed the straitjacket of totalitarian controls, it becomes more tolerant of religious sentiments in its midst. At the same time, however, the process of secularization at work in Soviet society fosters the attrition of the political faith which has provided the regime with its claim to legitimacy, its raison d'être. In the long run this process may yet prove to be a greater danger to the survival of the dictatorship than religion itself.

ROBERT A. FELDMESSER

The Political Consequences of Equality

The author of this selection is an Associate Professor of Sociology at Dartmouth College, where he specializes in the study of Soviet social stratification, education, and Marxian doctrine. He has twice been a research associate at Harvard University's Russian Research Center, and was formerly a recipient of a postdoctoral grant in Slavic studies from the Social Science Research Council. Professor Feldmesser obtained his first-hand experience of Soviet society through visits to the Soviet Union in 1956 and 1966.

A GREAT DEAL HAS BEEN WRITTEN on the emergence of gross inequalities of wealth, privilege, and official honor in Soviet society. The process, fully described and documented, may be said to have begun with a famous speech by Stalin in 1931, in which he denounced "equality-mongering" in the wage structure and called for a new

From Robert A. Feldmesser, "Equality and Inequality under Khrushchev," *Problems of Communism* (March-April, 1960), pp. 31–39. Reprinted by permission of the United States Information Agency.

attitude of "solicitude" toward the intelligentsia; it manifested itself in highly differentiated incomes, in a change in the composition of the Communist Party, in the establishment of tuition fees and other more subtle obstacles to higher education, in elegant uniforms and elaborate titles, and in a host of other ways. By the end of World War II, and particularly during the last years of Stalin's life, the trend was clear: the Soviet Union was well advanced along a seemingly irreversible course toward a rigid system of social stratification, in which the upper classes would remain upper, the lower classes lower, and the twain would rarely meet.

Yet the irreversible has now been reversed. With that breathtaking facility which so often startles us, the Soviet leadership has launched a series of measures calculated to reduce the degree and rigidity of differentiation in Soviet society to a very considerable extent. Many observers have not yet fully apprehended this turn of events, if only because all its component parts had not been assembled in one place: to do so is one objective of the present study. But partly, too, the lack of comprehension is due to a reluctance to credit Soviet leaders with the desire or ability to achieve so "virtuous" an aim as social equality—or rather, it is due to a failure to appreciate the *meaning* of equality in the Soviet system. A second objective here is to define that meaning.

The "Revival of Democracy"

[He] began to trample crudely on the methods of collectivity in leadership . . . to order people around and push aside the personnel of Soviet and economic organizations . . . [He] decided questions great and small by himself, completely ignoring the opinions of others.

[He] flattered himself with the belief that all [improvements] were due only to his own merits. The more successfully things went, the more conceited he became, the more airs he gave himself.

You get the impression that everything other people do is bad, and only the things [he] does are good.

These scathing remarks could well have been taken from Khrushchev's secret speech to the 20th Congress of the CPSU exposing the incredible extremes to which Stalin's method of one-man rule had gone. A common reaction to this speech abroad was to see

in it a confirmation of the trend toward inequality. The intelligentsia, or the "state bourgeoisie," despite their privileges *vis-à-vis*
other elements of the population, had long resented the Stalinist
tyranny. Now, as a result of their increasing power in an industrialized
and militarized state, they had reached the point where they could
force Khrushchev to confess that they had been unjustly treated,
to promise them the freedom of decision-making, and to guarantee
the security of their status.

Subsequent comments in the Soviet press have belied this interpretation. The quotations do not come from the secret speech; they
are attacks on, respectively, a *raion* party secretary, the chairman
of a city soviet executive committee, and a factory director. For,
as it now appears, the secret speech was directed not only at the
one big Stalin, but also at all the other little Stalins who had
grown up in his image. It has been followed up not with praise
for Soviet administrators, but with denunciations of "admin-
istrirovanie"—the high-handed, arrogant ways of officials who
have exercised "petty tutelage" over their subordinates; who have
glossed over short-comings, suppressed criticism, and persecuted
their critics; who have been "inattentive to the workers and their
needs"; who have, in short, violated the letter of Soviet law and
the spirit of "communist morality."

Denunciations of this sort are not, of course, a new phenomenon;
but what is interesting today is not only the frequency of such
attacks but the implicit admission that the inspiration for bad administrative habits came from very high up. Accordingly, Khrushchev's own behavior, so sharply at variance with Stalin's, has been
held up as an example for others to follow: Soviet officials have been
urged to get closer to the people, to pay more attention to them,
and not to rely exclusively on existing channels of authority.
Sessions of local soviets are being held more frequently; there have
been occasional reports of ministers and department heads being
subjected to questioning by deputies; in some instances, agendas of
meetings have been posted and public hearings held on the items
under discussion. The number of deputies in local soviets has been
increased by 1,800,000, and unpaid activists have been taking on
tasks formerly performed by the executive staff—as if housewives
were indeed to run the state. Along the same lines, there has been
a large-scale effort to reinvigorate the system of worker and
peasant correspondents, to protect them from reprisals by the
targets of their criticism, and to have them do more of the news-

papers' work in place of the professional journalistic staff. A party journal has told *raion* newspapers that they were not limited to criticizing "only rank-and-file workers and 'second-rank' officials of *raion* organizations."

The appeal for "popular participation" to reform the deeply ingrained bureaucratic habits of Soviet officialdom has even been extended to the party-controlled trade unions, which have been urged to shake off their submissiveness to factory executives and to offer vigorous opposition when necessary. Instances of rambunctious local trade-union committees have been held up for emulation, and workers enjoined to criticize "without being afraid that it will upset some director or other," and without having their remarks "prepared" or "cleared" by higher authorities.

Another indication of the new spirit, antedating the 20th Congress, has been the abolishment of the uniforms, insignia or rank, and titles which had been authorized for many civilian occupations during and after the war. There has been an appeal for more informal relations and less social distance between those of high rank and those of low, and for an end to such practices in the armed forces as separate dining rooms for the several ranks.

In general, the party seems to have been going out of its way to assert its respect for "ordinary" workers and peasants, a development reminiscent, as are many aspects of this campaign, of the attitude prevailing during the first decade after the October Revolution. Reversing a trend of more than 20 years' duration, the party has made a deliberate attempt to recruit more workers and peasants into its ranks: so much so, that Khrushchev was able to report at the 21st Congress that two-thirds of current admissions were in those categories, a figure which he accurately called a "considerable increase." In addition, the Soviet press has published numerous editorials, articles, and letters passionately proclaiming the honor and worth of manual labor in a socialist society, filled with glowing words about citizens who are not afraid of soiling their hands, who are "creating material values for the people," rather than "sitting in offices and filing papers." While this line of propaganda is not new, it has never been pursued so intensely. Indeed, it almost appears that the traditional trinity of "workers, collective farmers, and intelligentsia" has been replaced by a duad of the first two classes, so great has been the new stress on the "Soviet toilers."

The rights and privileges mentioned thus far may seem to be

only honorific. To be sure, they do not signify any real diffusion of the locus of power in Soviet society. Nevertheless, their importance should not be underrated: they do, after all, attempt to raise the ordinary worker's self-respect, and to imbue him with the consciousness—denied to him under Stalin—of his own contribution to the country's industrial progress. Having for years been exposed to harassment, incessant exhortations, and an attitude on the part of the authorities bordering on contempt, he is not likely to scorn even this—however mild—token of recognition and respect.

ADJUSTMENTS IN THE INCOME STRUCTURE

In any event, more tangible rewards have also resulted from the new policy. Although we need not take too literally all of the promises made by Khrushchev—and by Malenkov before him—to increase the output of consumers' goods, there is every indication that the lowest-paid Soviet workers and peasants have been placed in a better competitive position to buy whatever is available.

On the one hand, minimum wages were raised in 1956, and two more increases scheduled in the current plan will bring the wage floor up to 500–600 rubles[1] a month by 1965—hardly a level of luxury, but approximately twice what it is now; raises have also been promised to "medium-paid workers and employees." Old-age and disability pensions have been increased, too. Income taxes have been revised in favor of the lowest income brackets.

On the other hand, there has been a good deal of talk, and some action, aimed at reducing the incomes of managerial and scientific personnel. In particular, the awarding of lavish bonuses to administrative, party, and other officials has been repeatedly attacked, and it is almost certain that the worst abuses are being corrected, "voluntarily" if not otherwise. A decree of the Council of Ministers has warned against excessive expense accounts on *komandirovki* (business trips)—another common source of added income for economic staffs. Sputniks notwithstanding, the scientists have come in for their share of criticism, too, for holding multiple jobs and for receiving high incomes "merely" because they have higher degrees. . . .

RURAL REMEDIES

Even more striking have been the changes in the agricultural sector. Adjustments in crop-purchase prices and agricultural taxes

[1] Old rubles. Currently one new ruble is worth 10 old rubles, or $1.05 U.S.

and other steps taken since 1953 have raised the income of collective farmers in general while diminishing the range of earnings among and within the collectives. On several occasions, Khrushchev has referred to the "excessively high incomes" of some collective farms (as he has to the "unjustifiably high incomes" of some workers). One remedy, analogous to the industrial wage reform, has been the establishment of a uniform pricing system for agricultural purchases, without bonuses for exceeding the purchase plan, with the result, according to Khrushchev, that "many collective farms will undoubtedly get more, while the leading collective farms will receive . . . somewhat less than now. And this," he added, "will be entirely fair." Especially interesting is his implicit denial of the principle laid down by Stalin in 1931: that wide income differentials were needed as incentives to raise production. Khrushchev, on the contrary, has asserted that the farms with low income due to poor production are discouraged from increasing their output:

> . . . Collective farms that did not achieve the planned harvest . . . were penalized, as it were. . . . This, of course, did not spur them on. . . . The goal here must be a more correct determination of pay . . . in order to provide incentive not only to the leading but to all collective farms. . . .

IS THE CLASSLESS SOCIETY COMING?

The scope and force of the trend away from extreme differentiation are unmistakable. There are many clues other than those which have already been cited: criticism of the practice of assigning chauffeured cars to officials; a pervasive, if still partial, change in the method of awarding medals and orders; a demand that the Soviet fashion journal concern itself less with evening gowns and furs and more with "everyday" clothes. To dismiss all this evidence as mere window-dressing, as ritual obeisance to an ideology, explains nothing; for why is it happening *now*? Why should Khrushchev feel compelled to renew rituals that Stalin had long neglected, rituals that offend the sensibilities of the "elite"? What, then, does account for the change? Is one facet of the "transition to communism" to be the end of class distinctions?

Stalin, it seems clear, had felt that a high degree of differentiation was necessary to achieve his overriding goal—a very rapid process of industrialization subject to his absolute control. This meant, in the first place, that a group of loyal and competent administrators and other brain-workers had to be created, and quickly. It also meant that large segments of the population would have to be deprived, at least "temporarily," of material returns from their labor, in order that greater proportions of production could be applied to the expansion of industrial capacity. The consequently depressed condition of the workers and peasants Stalin sought to turn to good purpose, by offering them great rewards for joining the administrative and technical corps—hence the wealth, privilege, and prestige which came to define the upper end of the occupational hierarchy. The need for upward mobility to escape a life of privation would induce people to strive for educational training and vocational achievement, and would encourage obedience to Stalin's dictates, while the chance for upward mobility would serve as a substitute for the more prosaic benefits of a slow and moderate rise in the general standard of living.

The gap thus generated between the higher statuses and the lower ably served Stalin's purposes in some respects. Those in high positions came to live a different kind of life, free from the material anxieties of those over whom they stood. They became, in short, "insulated" from the less fortunate: blind or indifferent to the needs and wishes of the masses. For they learned that success was to be had by winning the favor not of those below them but of those above them, which was exactly what Stalin wanted them to learn. . . .

THE PROBLEMS OF STALINIST POLICY

Nevertheless, extreme social differentiation had its less desirable aspects, too. For one thing, it "over-motivated" the population: anything less than a higher education, and the higher occupation it brought, was regarded as a disgrace for an upper-status child and as a sad fate for a lower-status child—hence, the intense pressure exerted on the educational institutions, the reluctance of youths to commit themselves to factory jobs. For another and more important thing, it interfered with the operation of the impersonal selection system necessary to an efficient economy and to the reward-function of upward mobility. Those in higher and better paid positions were able to use their influence and their money to assure similar places for their children, at the expense of potentially more capable or more loyal children from less-favored families. Perhaps even worse, some children from well-to-do families neither studied nor worked, but lived off their parents' income—an idle existence which not only meant a loss to the labor force but also, if the Soviet press is to be believed, led in many cases to alcoholism, crime, or even to the acceptance of "bourgeois ideology."

This excessive measure of status security perverted adults as well as children. Once a man was granted local power, he was able to suppress or punish, if not ignore, criticism from his inferiors, and he cooperated with his colleagues to evade the regime's cross-checks on him. This had been intermittently acknowledged in the Soviet Union under the label of *semeistvennost* ("family-ness"), but the full dimensions of the problem are only now being revealed. Among many instances, one may be cited concerning the chairman of a city soviet executive committee who "forbade his assistants and the heads of the city executive committee departments to appeal to party organs without his consent." Thus, higher authorities were precluded from receiving the information they needed to keep tabs on their own subordinates. Or, if the party did manage to find out about and remove some incompetent or dishonest official, he often reappeared in another responsible position—partly, at least, as the result of friendships formed and mutual obligations exacted. Indeed, an integral part of the pattern has been the concern of officials to find places in the *apparat* for friends and relatives who could reciprocally provide a haven if necessary.

All of this was simply the obverse side of the arbitrary power delegated to local officials, for the sake of allowing them to carry out their instructions from above without interference from below. But it was ironically self-defeating: by being freed of criticism from below, administrators were able to free themselves of supervision from above. This threatened to contravene the cardinal dogma of the Soviet system, which has come to be known as Stalinism though it could as well be called Leninism or Khrushchevism: that ultimate power belongs exclusively to the party—or, more accurately, to the head of the party. Whenever any group jeopardizes that principle, it must be struck down, and that is what Khrushchev is doing. Stalin, in other words, forgot his Stalinism; and Khrushchev is not repudiating Stalinism, he is, if anything, reinstating it.

KHRUSHCHEV'S TWO-SIDED TASK

No doubt, the Soviet press, in characteristic fashion, has exaggerated the threat. Stalin was not a complete fool, and when all is said and done, he does seem to have kept things pretty well under control. If the group whose growth he fostered was an "elite," then surely no elite has ever proved so utterly helpless in preventing actions which, like those at present, so adversely affect it. The danger was a distant cloud—but a good Bolshevik tries not to wait until the storm has swept away his fortifications. Khrushchev's task, then, is to rid the "state bourgeoisie" of its cockiness, to disabuse it of the notion that it is safe whatever it does, to infuse into it fresh blood, personnel more responsive to orders. Just because of the kinds of positions these people occupy, the task will not be easy, and the plan may be "underfulfilled." But given the Soviet political structure, the odds are on Khrushchev's side.

The nature of the targets at which Khrushchev has taken aim makes his crusade sound like an echo of earlier revolutionary periods; but in actuality, the development does not connote a return to the situation that prevailed in the early 1920's, for Khrushchev has learned something from Soviet history. The extremes of high and low incomes are to be moderated—but "equality-mongering" is still wrong. Mass participation and criticism from below are to be permitted—but not "violations of state discipline" or "slander of the party and its leaders." Executives should be more humble, more attentive to their subordinates—but the principle of "one-man management" is to be preserved. "The struggle against the cult of the individual does not at all mean a belittling of the significance of leadership and leaders. . . . The party does not advocate the denial of authorities." Moreover, Khrushchev has expressly defended the nonmanual pursuits—"those who work in offices are not at all bureaucrats; they are the creative people who originate that which is new . . ."—and he has strongly implied that, even under communism, there will still be the bosses and the bossed: communist society will be "highly organized." Complete equality is not just around the corner, nor even being contemplated.

"CLASSLESSNESS" DEFINED

Nevertheless, Khrushchev *is* seeking a classless society, in the proper sense of the term. If an "upper class," for example, means anything, it means a group of people who share fairly distinctive values and advantages which they are able to hold on to for some length of time, even against the resistance of others. Yet in the totalitarian scheme of things, it is essential to the preservation of party supremacy that no group become so intrenched in positions of strength as to become insulated against further demands from the party. An "upper class," or any other "class," is no more admissible than an autonomous trade union or ethnic group. Hence the party must insist—in the long run—that every man be individually and continuously on trial, that status and rewards remain contingent and ephemeral. The greatest threat to the party is the development of a sense of identification or solidarity within a group—or class—and this is precisely what was happening to the Soviet elite. Khrushchev's war against the bourgeoisie is, in fact, only an extension of the battle with the bureaucrats which has long been a part of Soviet policy, even if it was sometimes muted. In short, "classlessness" is essentially a corollary of Stalinism.

PETER VIERECK

The Intellectuals' Challenge to Party Control

Peter Viereck has written a number of books and articles on problems of ideology in modern society, and has won both Tietzens and Pulitzer prizes for his poetry as well. Professor of Modern European and Russian History at Mount Holyoke College, he has made two extensive visits to the Soviet Union, in 1961 as a Visiting Professor with the Russian-American Cultural Exchange Program, and in 1962 as a resident scholar sponsored by the Twentieth Century Fund.

A PENDULUM BETWEEN thaw and freeze characterizes not only Soviet society today but Russian society through the ages. Thus a reformist Alexander I seems forever alternating with a dogmatist Nicholas I, a reformist Alexander II with a dogmatist Alexander III, a reformist Kerensky with a dogmatist Lenin, the N. E. P. thaw of the mid-1920's with Stalin. And already before Alexander I, there was the pro-western "18th century enlightenment" of Catherine the Great alternating with the anti-western dogmatist Paul. The pendulum is not

From Peter Viereck, "The Mob Within the Heart," *Tri-Quarterly* (Spring, 1965), pp. 7-19. Reprinted by permission of the *Tri-Quarterly*.

automatic. It is not swung by a capitalized attraction called "History" or by any other intellectual or economic determinism. It is swung only by concrete human beings, making efforts of will and conviction in either direction. Yet it is reasonable to assume that both directions will continue to be actively and effectively represented. For both directions have deep roots in Russia's past and present and are being personally passed on to the future. . . .

Equally rejecting American pessimism (which expects "a new Stalinist terror" after Khrushchev's downfall) and American optimism (which expects "liberalism at last" after his downfall) here follow some of the reasons for a more balanced, cautious optimism. One is probably justified in expecting more cultural (but not political) liberty from Khrushchev's successors. The increase in cultural and intellectual liberty (Lysenko's downfall, for example, followed Khrushchev's) seems inevitable not because of any sudden conversion to John Stuart Mill on the part of this tough, cynical new "collective leadership" but because of changes in Soviet society as a whole.

What has saved the Soviet rebel writers of today from Stalin-style torture and death? No mere change of rulers. Khrushchev, Brezhnev, Kosygin (also Mikoyan, Suslov, Podgorny) all made their careers under Stalin; all had once actively helped his lethal purges. Yet Soviet writers have not been suffering in the 1960's, under Khrushchev-Brezhnev-Kosygin and their cultural watchdog Ilychev, the consequences they would have suffered in that earlier decade when the same Ilychev was still one of Stalin's favorite editors. In December 1962 and March 1963 the official language of Khrushchev and Ilychev, darkly threatening the experimental painters and revisionist poets, resembled the language of Stalin and Zhdanov in 1949. Yet the consequences for the victims have been incomparably less dire than under Stalin and Zhdanov.

The most denounced of these victims—the poets Voznesensky and Yevtushenko, the prose writers Ehrenburg, Aksyonov, and Victor Nekrasov—are not only still alive but out of prison. They are still publishing widely without major concessions. So far, none has been expelled from the Writers Union, despite threats to that effect by Government leaders (notably against the unrecanting Nekrasov). It may be evidence for bad nerves among watchdogs that the vast public poetry readings in Moscow, which I witnessed in 1961, 1962, and 1963, are no longer permitted. But smaller indoor readings by the denounced poets continue to express and fan the fervor of students for freer self-expression. Yevtushenko is still listed on the masthead of *Yunost* ("Youth"), from which the Party had threatened to oust him.

Since there have been no sweeping changes in Stalinist personnel nor in the official language and aim of ideological control and since, nevertheless, the Stalinist consequences no longer occur, the change must be in Soviet life itself. "Soviet life" is a vague phrase at best, a matter of atmosphere, and yet a real source of hope for Russia, for American relations with Russia, and for the cause of peace. The new atmosphere may be partly summarized by observing that Pavlov's dog never had an education. Therefore, he stayed conditioned. Not so the newly educated Russian of today. No longer can he be disregarded by the Party as a "dumb muzhik." No longer will he stand for what he had to endure in Stalin's day. A separate factor may be noted now but analyzed later: the feeling of guilt and atonement in a certain limited number of ex-Stalinists.

Within this improved way of life, the old historical pendulum continues to alternate, just as much as before. But now less murderously. And quicker, more deviously: for example, one could write whole books—and the best authorities do—tracing how Yevtushenko was ousted during the 1963 freeze from the governing board of the Moscow Writers Union but was re-elected to it in January 1965, or tracing how the last volume of Ehrenburg's memoirs was announced by the thaw magazine, *Novy Mir*, for 1964 publication and then mysteriously failed to appear, only to be re-announced all over again by *Novy Mir* for 1965. To become a virtuoso of "thawmanship" (a word we may coin to express in literature what "Kremlinology" expresses in politics) one must ponder the secret meaning, if any, of why (for example) the January *Yunost* of 1965 failed to print a certain long-announced new poem of Yevtushenko's; does it perhaps mean a new reversal of that third rehabilitation which followed his third disgrace? But all such reversals can again be reversed, and every book and article of thawmanship must revise its galley proofs frantically to be one-up on rival experts. No end to this; and up to a reasonable point, necessary. But at some point of diminishing returns, it becomes not only simpler but truer to utter instead the single word "pendulum". . . .

Will the Government's limited and manipulated de-Stalinization get out of hand and create an uncheckable thirst for freedom? Yes and no. Probably yes in regard to the broad-based demand of all classes for a freer private life. Probably no in regard to those basic democratic liberties which are taken for granted in much

of the West but which have not yet become sufficiently rooted
in modern Russia (except for the 1905–17 Duma interlude) to produce a broad-based demand. Moreover, these democratic liberties
are incompatible with the economic privileges of the one-party
ruling class (as well as with its priestly psychological privileges
as the official Caesaro-papist guardians of absolute truth) and will
be ruthlessly restricted by any Communist government, no matter
how anti-Stalinist, except for minor non-basic concessions.

Russia's irresistible future expansion of the private life—
that is, of cultural and human liberties—is partly compatible
with one-party control of politics and economics; that is, with
the present more authoritarian than totalitarian dictatorship.
(Only Stalin and Hitler were true totalitarians: Mussolini, Franco,
all the present Communist dictatorships except perhaps China, and
most of South America are neither totalitarian nor free but authoritarian.) The partial compatibility between cultural freedom and
complete Communist political dictatorship is proved by the current
practice in Poland, Hungary, Yugoslavia. Inside those countries
I found that their boast of having more cultural freedom than
Russia is not a myth but a reality; visit their theaters and cafes,
or their very individualistic farmhouses, or pick up any of their
magazines and newspapers, and the difference is self-evident. When
these three Communist governments allow this greater cultural
freedom (with which Russia will have to catch up), their motive
is partly a yielding to the inevitable and partly an astute exploitation of the inevitable. Why exploitation? Because their partial
cultural freedom, by serving as a safety valve for man's irrepressible
individualism, often struck me as—in the short run—strengthening
rather than weakening the Communist dictatorship in political and
economic terms.

So much for the short run. In the long run will the new cultural
momentum for non-political liberty remain safety-valved—or
canalized—within the Communist framework (a framework sincerely
accepted by Russia's literary rebels but not by Poland's)? Or
will such cultural momentum spill over into political momentum?
It is easier to raise than to answer these questions. There are
too many interacting factors (and we ourselves are part of the test
tube we are trying to see from the outside) to enable us to answer
these questions confidently. Or to enable the Communist leaders
to answer them. Hence, the zigzag in the cultural policies of the
various Communist dictatorships. Such a course is probably due

not to diabolical master-plans but to genuine confusion, uncertainty, and inconsistency at the top about these unanswerable questions, which certainly confuse us as well. . . .

In a pro-Castro poem appearing October 22, 1962 in *Pravda*, Yevtushenko declares: a free debate between rival schools of culture—he names only socialist realism versus abstract art but implies free cultural self-expression in general—can well be accompanied by the Communist one-party state in politics. According to the poem, the two schools of artists drop their rival paint-brushes to pick up their shared political rifles whenever capitalist imperialism threatens to attack. This example sustains our thesis that Western optimists err in expecting political freedom from the thaw movement but that Western pessimists err in overlooking the freedom brought by the thaw movement into other areas: cultural freedom and the self-expression of the human heart. The boulevardier Ehrenburg, the aesthete Voznesensky, the sober Communist war-hero Tvardovsky, the lone Prometheus Nekrasov, and the tribal medicine-man Yevtushenko may differ on many other issues. But these five most active voices of the thaw do share two inarticulate goals: a revolution and a restoration. Let us dare to articulate the inarticulate, by summarizing their two shared goals somewhat like this: (1) a non-Communist revolution of feelings, on behalf of the non-monolithic private life in heart and art; (2) a Communist restoration of "Leninism," on behalf of the monolithic public life in politics and economics. Their second goal contains (as Lenin would say) contradictions. For the real Lenin probably lacked those more human, less ideological and less technocratic qualities they attribute to "Leninism."

Russia's momentum for political liberty is feeble, but here is a possibility that would strengthen it and thereby threaten Communist rule. It is the possibility that one of Khrushchev's successors may try to halt too long, in its repressive phase, the cultural pendulum between thaw and freeze, thereby forcing as a counter-reaction the spilling over of cultural momentum into political momentum. This will not necessarily happen; for in Russia the two momentums are separate—they are not a single overlapping freedom as in the West—and only the frustration of Russia's very strong and unhaltable cultural momentum can arouse Russia's very weak momentum for the political kind of freedom. World Communists share with world anti-communists a belief in greater cultural freedom for artists than Russia now permits. Thus the Italian

and even the French Communist Parties have refused to accept the
Moscow persecution of abstract art even while accepting Moscow's
far bloodier political persecutions (like the suppression of Hungary).
The strength of the cultural momentum even in Russia, the feebleness
of the political momentum *especially* in Russia—both kinds of
freedom desirable but in Russia not equally attainable—are the
two most vivid impressions remaining from my many months behind
the Iron Curtain. In culture and intelligence Russians are our
equals; in pluralist flexibility and easy-going tolerance they are
our inferiors; in wisdom, that intuitive human wisdom which only
suffering can earn, they are our superiors.

When I asked Ilya Ehrenburg what guarantee there was against a
return to Stalinism in view of the absence of any Russian movement for political liberty (free constitution, free press, free elections)
and in view of the continuance of the one-party dictatorship,
he replied: "The guarantee lies not in a constitution or in political
institutions nor in the whim of governing individuals but in the
new knowledge and strength of the Russian people themselves.
For the first time in Russian history the people has become"
(we were speaking in French) "*mûr.*"

Hence my cautious optimism about the future changes of Russian
cultural and intellectual freedom: not because I trust the intentions of the Party bosses, who are never going to allow free elections or any freedom threatening the Communist framework, but
because I trust the new maturity of the younger generation of
workingmen as well as intellectuals, who will demand and often get
every concession possible within the framework.

All such gains, limited but far from phoney, succeed precisely
because they never smash the Communist framework itself. (In
contrast with Poland, no Russian writer I talked to wants to go
outside that framework or restore what they rather vaguely and
anachronistically call "capitalism.") The present dictatorship,
harassed by Party dissensions at home and abroad and facing the
two fronts of literary revisionists and Chinese dogmatists, simply
lacks that monolithic strength which enabled Stalin to ignore
popular pressures and to send 15,000,000 inconvenient citizens
into slave labor camps. Most observers I met, many of them Party
members, agreed that the Zhdanov days cannot be repeated and that
the Party itself will ultimately have to put up with a lot more
cultural independence.

Suggestions for Further Reading

The democratic nature of the contemporary Soviet state is a question subject to widely diverse opinions. The strongest optimistic statements come, naturally, from Soviet sources and from Marxists in Western countries. For the former, see O. V. Kuusinen et al., *Fundamentals of Marxism–Leninism* (Moscow: Foreign Languages Publishing House, 1963); and V. Kotok, *The Soviet Representative System* (Moscow: Progress Publishers, n.d.). The most far–reaching Soviet statement on the future of Soviet society is the "Program of the Communist Party of the Soviet Union (1961)," translated and annotated by Herbert Ritvo, in *The New Soviet Society* (New York: The New Leader, 1962). The Western Marxist view is represented by Giuseppe Boffa, *Inside the Khrushchev Era* (Rome: Marzani and Munsell, 1959); and Herbert Aptheker, ed., *Marxism and Democracy* (New York: Humanities Press, 1965). Arthur Adams, a non–Marxist Western scholar, presents a moderate positive view. He sees "some degree of democracy emerging in the Soviet Union, both within the Communist Party and within the governmental apparatus." See his "Democratic Ferment Behind the Curtain," *The Progressive* (August, 1962), pp. 13–15.

The focus of less optimistic analyses is the Communist Party's continued domination of political progress, which affords little influence to the Soviets, the public organizations, or the people themselves. In discussing the Party Program for 1961, Ivo Lapenna concludes that "the role of the soviets will remain approximately as insignificant as it was before the Twenty–Second Congress." See his "Party and State in the Programme," in Leonard Schapiro, *The USSR and the Future* (New York: Praeger, 1962). For supporting views see Leonard Schapiro, "The Party and the State," in Walter Lacqueur and Leopold Labedz, eds., *The Future of the Communist Society* (New York: Praeger, 1962).

Within the Party itself, significant changes are taking place in the relations among the major organs, in the processes of deliberation and decision–making, and in the positions of individual leaders. Carl A. Linden, *Khrushchev and the Soviet Leadership, 1957–1964* (Baltimore: Johns Hopkins Press, 1966) analyzes perceptively the conflict and instability of the ruling elite under

Khrushchev's leadership. For a similar treatment which also includes material on the new post-Khrushchev leadership, see Robert
Conquest, *Russia After Khrushchev* (New York: Praeger, 1965).
Myron Rush considers the problem of transferring leadership in
his *Political Succession in the USSR* (New York: Columbia University Press, 1965). For a useful collection of documents and an
interpretative commentary on this subject, see Howard Swearer,
The Politics of Succession in the USSR (Boston: Little, Brown,
1964). A recent series of articles in *Problems of Communism*
(January/February, 1966 through July/August, 1967) presents
several differing viewpoints of the role of the Communist Party
evolving since Khrushchev's ouster. The lead article in this discussion is Zbigniew Brzezinski, "The Soviet Political System:
Transformation or Degeneration" (January/February, 1966). On the
same topic, see also John Armstrong, "Party Bifurcation and Elite
Interests," *Soviet Studies* (April, 1966), pp. 417–430.

The process of liberalization necessarily involves an increase in
the political importance of non-party groups and institutions.
There are as yet, however, very few general studies of the interest
group as a separate political force—partly, no doubt, because
there is little available data. Two recent attempts to deal with
this topic are Barbara Green, "Soviet Politics and Interest Groups,"
Current History (October, 1966), pp. 213–217; and Gordon Skilling,
"Interest Groups and Communist Politics," *World Politics* (April,
1966), pp. 435–451. (The latter deals with Eastern Europe as well
as the Soviet Union.) Studies of the political role of individual
groups are far more numerous, and only a few can be mentioned
here: Jeremy R. Azrael, *Managerial Power and Soviet Politics*
(Cambridge: Harvard University Press, 1966); Sidney I. Ploss,
Conflict and Decision-Making in Soviet Russia (Princeton: Princeton University Press, 1965), dealing with agricultural groups;
David Granick, *The Red Executive: A Study of the Organization
Man in Russian Industry* (Garden City: Doubleday, 1960); Ray-
mond L. Garthoff, "The Role of the Military in Post-Stalin
Politics" (Santa Monica: RAND Corporation Research Memoran-
dum P-937, Sept. 12, 1956); and D. Richard Little, "The Academy
of Pedagogical Sciences: Its Political Role," *Soviet Studies* (January,
1968).

Of all these groups, the literary intelligentsia has received the
most attention from Western scholars: it is this group that many
foresee as the most serious challenge to Soviet totalitarianism. The

struggle during the past decade between the regime and the liberal writers and artists is described by David Burg, "The 'Cold War' on the Literary Front," *Problems of Communism* (January/February, 1963), pp. 44–58; Merle Fainsod, "The Role of Intellectuals in the Soviet Union," *Texas Quarterly* (Winter, 1965), pp. 88–103; and Eugene Kamenka, "The 'Creative Intellectual' and the Soviet State," *Australian Outlook* (August, 1963), pp. 175–193. The general view of these authors is that young writers and artists are pressing the political elite more and more to relax their harsh controls on the arts, and that the regime is finding it more and more difficult to ignore or suppress them. An even more optimistic outlook is expressed by a young Yugoslav writer, Mihajlo Mihajlov (currently in jail in Belgrade), in his book *Moscow Summer* (New York: Farrar, Straus and Giroux, 1965). Mihajlov states that the "basic characteristic of the Soviet literary mood in the summer of 1964 was the expectation of a final liberation of literature and the arts from all possible restrictions of dogmatic Marxism." By contrast, a highly pessimistic view appears in Max Hayward and Leopold Labedz, "Writers and the Police," *Encounter* (January, 1966); and in Abraham Brumberg, "Traitors in the Dock," *Problems of Communism* (March/April, 1966), pp. 70–78.

The best work on recent reforms in the Soviet legal system is Harold Berman, *Justice in the USSR* (New York: Vintage, 1963). Some first-hand observations and an impressionistic interpretation of the Soviet court system are found in George Feifer, *Justice in Moscow* (New York: Simon and Schuster, 1964). The judicial functions of "public organizations" and other informal groups are discussed, in a rather gloomy light, by Abraham Brumberg, "When Comrades Sit in Judgment," *Problems of Communism* (March/April, 1965), pp. 140–144; and in A. Karavaev, "Humanism and Soviet Democracy," *Institute for the Study of the USSR Bulletin* (February, 1964), pp. 3–15. The "anti-parasite" legislation, introduced in the late 1950's, was widely viewed in the West as an extension of the Party's control over the behavior of citizens. This legislation is analyzed in Leon Lipson, "Hosts and Pests: the Fight Against Parasites," *Problems of Communism* (March/April, 1965), pp. 72–81; and in Albert Boiter, "Comradely Justice: How Durable Is It?," *ibid.*, pp. 82–92. Since the fall of Khrushchev, however, there has been what R. Beerman calls a "considerable liberalization of the former rather strict measure," in "The 'Anti-Parasite Law' of the RSFSR Modified," *Soviet Studies* (January, 1966), pp. 387–388.

Religious and cultural attachments of the Soviet population have long been the subject of intense concern by the Party leadership. The government's positive attempt to shape these beliefs through education and indoctrination has been supplemented by a massive campaign against all forms of belief and opinion contrary to the official ideology. For an explication of the government's anti-religious policies, see Harry Willetts, "De-opiating the Masses," *Problems of Communism* (November/December, 1964), pp. 32–41; P. B. Taylor, "Sectarians in Soviet Courts," *Russian Review* (July, 1965), pp. 278–288; and Michael Bourdeaux, *Opium of the People: The Christian Religion in the USSR* (Indianapolis: Bobbs–Merrill, 1966). An interesting symposium on the question of religion is presented in William C. Fletcher and Anthony J. Stover, eds., *Religion and the Search for New Ideals* (New York: Praeger, 1967).

The nationality problem is the subject of an entire issue of *Problems of Communism* (September/October, 1967). For more comprehensive studies of particular nationalities see Olaf Caroe, *Soviet Empire, the Turks of Central Asia and Stalinism* (New York: St. Martin's Press, 1967), a contrast to Alec Nove's and J. A. Newth's treatment of the same subject in *The Soviet Middle East, A Communist Model for Development* (New York: Praeger, 1967); Alexandre Bennigsen and Chantal Lemercier-Quelquejay, *Islam in the Soviet Union* (New York: Praeger, 1967); Robert S. Sullivant, *Soviet Politics and the Ukraine, 1917–1957* (New York: Columbia University Press, 1962); Ben Ami, *Between Hammer and Sickle* (Philadelphia: The Jewish Publication Society of America, 1967), on the status of Jews in the Soviet Union; and V. Stanley Vardys, *Lithuania Under the Soviets* (New York: Praeger, 1965).

Despite the government's antipathy toward national and religious separatism, the Soviet people has recently undergone a revival of belief and a search for new ideals, as a number of studies point out. P. Konstantinov discusses the revived interest in organized religion in "Orthodoxy and the Young Generation in the USSR," *Studies on the Soviet Union* (4, 1966), 24–34; and M. Klimenko, in "The Question of Religion in Modern Russian Literature," *Religion in Life* (Autumn, 1966), pp. 608–616. Other authors note a growing search for values outside of, or supplementary to, those of organized religion, for example, Harrison E. Salisbury, "Spiritual Stirrings in Russia," *A New Russia?* (New York: Harper and Row, 1962), pp. 75–86; and Peter Reddaway, "The Search for New Ideals in the USSR: Some First-Hand Impressions," *Studies on the Soviet Union* (4, 1966), pp. 83–90.

Reforms in the Soviet economy since the death of Stalin are analyzed in Alec Nove, *The Soviet Economy* (New York: Praeger, 1966) and Robert W. Campbell, *Soviet Economic Power* (Boston: Houghton Mifflin, 1966). The Liberman reforms in particular are discussed by Michael Kaser, "Kosygin, Liberman and the Pace of Soviet Development," *World Today* (September, 1965), pp. 375–388; and by Marshall Goldman, "Economic Revolution in the Soviet Union," *Foreign Affairs* (January, 1967), pp. 319–331. For the Soviet response to Western interpretations of the economic reforms, see L. Leontiev, "The Soviet Economic Reform and its Critics," Moscow *New Times* (November 24, 1965), pp. 3–5, and (December 1, 1965), pp. 12–14; and B. Rabitskii, "In Refutation of Bourgeois Interpretations of the Economic Reforms in the USSR," *Voprosy Ekonomiki* (Vol. 10, 1965), translated in *Problems of Economics* (March, 1966), pp. 21–31. The status of the consumer is debated by Immogene Erro and others in *Problems of Communism* (November/December, 1963, and July/August, 1964). For more recent developments, see Marshall Goldman, "Trade and the Consumer," *Survey* (July, 1967), pp. 129–142.

The 1967 celebration of the 50th anniversary of the Revolution has stimulated several useful general summaries of post–revolutionary developments in the Soviet Union. The July, 1967 issue of *Survey* is devoted entirely to an assessment of changes since 1917. See also the series of articles appearing in the New York *Times* intermittently between October 2 and November 3, 1967, and those in the *Christian Science Monitor,* appearing each Wed. between Sept. 27 and Nov. 29, 1967. Two other useful studies of this period are Allan Kassof, ed., *Prospects for Soviet Society* (New York: Praeger, 1967); and Samuel Hendel and Randolph L. Braham, *The USSR After 50 Years* (New York: Knopf, 1967). The Central Committee of the Soviet Communist Party marked the occasion by publishing a lengthy document entitled "Fiftieth Anniversary of the Great October Socialist Revolution: Theses of the CC of the CPSU," which traces the history of the Revolution and post–revolutionary developments from the perspective of the current party leadership. An English translation appears in *The Current Digest of the Soviet Press* (July 12 and 19, 1967). In response to this document, *Problems of Communism* printed a group of essays (November/December, 1967), intended to correct what the editors saw as the Soviet document's biased historical record. These two documents provide an interesting contrast in the presentation of the last fifty years of Soviet history.